Books Have Meant To My Life What the Sun Has Meant To the Planet Earth.

–Earl Nightingale

Michelle Buck
Free Enterprise Nov. 1986
Hyatt, Incline Village, Nev.

The People You Meet & The Books You Read

Books by Charles E. Jones

Life Is Tremendous
Motivational Classics
The Books You Read – Business Edition
The Books You Read – Devotional Edition
The Books You Read – Historical Edition

You are the same today
as you will be five years from now
except for two things–

The People You Meet and THE BOOKS You Read

edited by
Charles E. Jones

Foreword by
Og Mandino

Published by
Executive Books
P.O. Box 1044, Harrisburg PA 17108

Published by Executive Books
Box 1044
Harrisburg, PA 17108
(717) 763-1950

Printed in the United States of America

To

Jere

Pamela

Candace

Jeffrey

Tracey

Jamie

Foreword

by Og Mandino, CPAE

Several years ago, while on tour to promote one of my books, I was asked a question by a television talk show host that I hadn't heard before. After he had introduced me and I had taken my seat he held up a copy of my latest book and asked, "Og, what will this book do for me?"

I pondered for several moments and then replied, "It might not do anything for you. It's just a book . . . composed of a little ink, some wood pulp, and glue. If you take that book home tonight and read it expecting that your world will change for the better as soon as you finish, then you might as well have taken the money you spent on the book and thrown it away instead."

Unlike an aspirin, that one can take and then wait passively for the headache to disappear, a good book will do nothing for you if it is read with your eyes open but your mind and heart closed. Especially does this apply to books in the self-help and inspirational field. You are wasting your time and your money exploring this great area of literature unless you apply yourself differently when reading these classics than you would some light piece of adventure or romance or even the comic strips.

Let's say you have a problem and you recognize that you do. For example, you know that you just don't have a very high opinion of yourself and this gnawing self-doubt about your abilities is holding you back in both your personal and business life. Someone, a friend perhaps, also recognizing your problem, has suggested that you get yourself a copy of Maxwell Maltz's *Psycho-Cybernetics*. Now you are in your living room, sitting comfortably in your favorite chair, holding that great classic. Before you begin, you must convince yourself of one important fact . . . that Dr. Maltz knows a great deal more about rebuilding your self-image than you do. And, since your present way of life has not enjoyed much success, you are going to take the advice of this acknowledged expert and begin applying it to your life.

Now begin reading . . . with an open mind and a pen or pencil in your hand. Whenever you come upon a suggestion or an idea that you think might be beneficial to you, underline it. Read the entire book in this manner . . . and don't hurry. Speed reading may be great if you're trying to hurry through some report for a meeting in an hour but it won't do anything for you if you are trying to soak in advice that will make a permanent change in your life.

When you have finished with the book, put it aside for a few days. Then, pick it up and read it again. Yes, again. Nobody said this would be easy. On the second reading, you will be pleasantly surprised to note how much you missed on your first read-through. On this second trip you might want to limit yourself to a chapter a day. If it takes twenty days, so what? Isn't this extra effort worth it if you come out of the experience being a better salesperson, sales manager, coach, parent . . . or human being?

Many years ago, when I was just about as complete a failure as one can become, I began to spend a good deal of time in libraries, looking for some answers. Where had I gone wrong? How could I possibly have fouled up my life so badly? And, was it too late for me . . . a thirty-five year old wanderer with only a high school education?

I found all the answers I needed in that golden vein of ore that every library has, that special shelf of books devoted to success, how to achieve it, and how to hold on to it after one attains it. My counselors were some of the wisest people who have ever lived . . . people like Elbert Hubbard, Norman Vincent Peale, W. Clement Stone, Napoleon Hill, Dale Carnegie, Maxwell Maltz, Louis Binstock and Dorothea Brande. The advice from their books helped to change my life.

I read their words with an open mind and a burning desire to change . . . and I had nothing to lose by accepting their principles and applying them to a life that had been wasted up to that time. I owe them so very much and in every book I write I am still trying to repay my debt.

This marvelous book that you are now holding is unique . . . a shopping list, really, to guide you to the very best work that man and woman has written dealing with many areas of your life. Search these pages carefully and I am certain that you will discover exactly the book or books that will help you to deal with your specific problem, whatever it may be. Just think of the time alone that this precious reference will save you in your personal search for the answers you need in order to reach your full potential.

We all need help. There is no such thing as a self-made man or woman. Charles "Tremendous" Jones has performed a miracle through this book. He has created a vehicle, a Channel if you will, that will lead you to the perfect specialist that can cure whatever is preventing you from making the progress you deserve. You are a miracle, God's greatest miracle, and now you have a guide that will lead you to the answers you need and prove to yourself, as well as others, how great you really are. Happy hunting, good reading, and joyful living!

Contents

Great Thoughts On Books

A Book I'd Like to Share

Great Thoughts on Reading 253

Greats on Reading 258

Blakey-Burton

Ashley Montagu on Reading 259

Introduction

Every good thought, every good thing that has happened in my life is related directly or indirectly to a book. That should explain my motivation for this book. If I lived a million years, I could not repay the debt of gratitude I feel for those who invested their lives in writing and the many who thought enough of me to give me a book.

My management training began with a Sunday School class of young boys in 1950. My dear friend, Willard Niesen, gave me a book by Donald Grey Barnhouse. That book helped me enough that the boys were able to give me time to learn to teach.

My early business experience was one failure and discouragement after another. My boss, Bill Meckley, gave me a book by Paul Speicher that fueled my hopes and dreams. One line that I've never forgotten: "An attitude of gratitude flavors everything you do." I discovered through books that if you keep working and are thankful, success is inevitable.

Each of my children have been a blessing and a challenge. Only through the books we read together, that I gave them, or they discovered, did we weather the storms and become closer rather than drift further apart. Now I'm experiencing the same joy of closeness with my grandchildren through book reading and memorizing incentives.

It was through a severe physical crisis that lasted several months that I began to read with my heart and not just my mind. No drugs could have provided the 'high' of realizing all those wonderful truths that lay dormant in me awaiting words to frame the thoughts so I could think, share, and experience them.

Through books even success took on a different meaning when after exceeding all my financial dreams and pushing forty, I suddenly lost everything. The following years were agonizing, humiliating and frustrating. But because of books, those years became the most wonderful of my life. Books helped me to laugh at heartaches, concentrate on the essential, and be thankful in everything. Authors, Oswald Chambers and Watchman Nee, became my closest friends even though I had never met either one.

And finally my marriage. How wonderful it would be if all our courtship dreams would turn into reality following the marriage. Fortunately for Gloria and me, we were totally committed to each other, but we were still in different worlds. Books changed that too. One of my favorite authors is A. W. Tozer. As Gloria began to enjoy Tozer and many other beautiful books, our worlds became one.

I hope the books you discover through this book will enrich your life so tremendously that all who meet you will sense that you are a better person because of the books you've read. As you read remember:

Don't read to be big,
  Read to be down to earth.
Don't read to be smart,
  Read to be real.
Don't read to memorize,
  Read to realize.
Don't read to learn,
  Read to sometimes unlearn.
Don't read a lot,
  Read just enough to keep yourself curious and hungry, to learn more, to keep getting younger as you grow older.

–Charles E. Jones

Great Thoughts On Books

The Joy of Books

by Alfred Montapert
Author, Business Executive

In a well-furnished library, we possess the power to call upon the minds of the greatest men who ever existed. We can question Xenophon and Caesar on their campaigns, make Demosthenes and Cicero plead before us, join in the audiences of Socrates and Plato, and receive demonstrations from Euclid, Shakespeare and Newton. In books we have the choicest thoughts of the ablest men in their best dress.

To any lover of books the very mention of these names brings back a crowd of delicious memories, grateful recollections of peaceful home hours, after the labors and anxieties of the day. How thankful we ought to be for these wonderful blessings, for this numberless host of friends who never weary, betray, or forsake us!

Most of those who have written in praise of books have thought they could say nothing more conclusive than to compare them to friends. "All men," said Socrates, "have their different objects of ambition . . . horses, dogs, money, honor, as the case may be; but for his own part he would rather have a good friend than all these put together."

Life is not merely to live, but to live well!

Aroused by Books

by Anatole Broyard
Author–Critic

I feel that every time I open a book, I risk my life – my conception of my life – and having survived some three hundred such experiences in the past three years, I think I can safely recommend the adventure. In fact, books may be our best cure for what Baudelaire called the quotidian frenzy. Recently, there has been a rash of true stories about people who threw up everything and went to live in the woods to get away from it all. I have found that getting *into* it all is a far better defense against the onslaught of our age. When you know what you're up against, you feel better about it. In some cases, you may even want to press closer.

It may sound as if I'm talking exclusively about nonfiction books – state of the union analysis of the American soul – but I believe that fiction, poetry, books on art, *any* kind of book can have an equal effect. Every work of the imagination offers another view of life, an invitation to spend a few days inside somebody else's emotions. And if the book is any good, you won't escape unscathed.

I've gravitated toward books that betrayed at least an ambivalent affection for our faltering institutions and their victims. In my experience, authors who lack even the most grudging feeling of attachment for the country they live in are as arrested in their development as people who proudly proclaim that they hate their mothers and fathers.

Thoughts about Books

Books are the legacies that a great genius leaves to mankind, which are delivered down from generation to generation, as presents to the posterity of those who are yet unborn.

–Joseph Addison

A good book is the precious life-blood of a master spirit, embalmed and treasured up on purpose to a life beyond life.

–John Milton

All that Mankind has done, thought, gained or been, it is lying as in magic preservation in the pages of Books. They are the chosen possession of men.

–Thomas Carlyle

A man's reading program should be as carefully planned as his daily diet, for that too is food, without which he cannot grow mentally.

–Andrew Carnegie

The choice of books, like that of friends, is a serious duty. We are responsible for what we read as what we do.

–John Lubbock

C. S. Lewis on Old Books

The student is half afraid to meet one of the great philosophers face to face. He feels himself inadequate and thinks he will not understand him. But if he only knew, the great man, just because of his greatness, is much more intelligible than his modern commentator. The simplest student will be able to understand, if not all, yet a very great deal of what Plato said; but hardly anyone can understand some modern books on Platonism. It has always therefore been one of my main endeavours as a teacher to persuade the young that first-hand knowledge is not only more worth acquiring than second-hand knowledge, but is usually much easier and more delightful to acquire.

This mistaken preference for the modern books and this shyness of the old ones is nowhere more rampant than in theology. Wherever you find a little study circle of Christian laity you can be almost certain that they are studying not St. Luke or St. Paul or St. Augustine or Thomas Aquinas or Hooker or Butler, but Mr. Berdyaev or Mr. Maritain or Mr. Niebuhr or Miss Sayers or even myself.

Now this seems to me topsy-turvy. Naturally, since I myself am a writer, I do not wish the ordinary reader to read no modern books. But if he must read only the new or only the old, I would advise him to read the old.

God in the Dock, 1970

Goodbye, Books

a rhyme which has been written in many a book–

"If thou art borrowed by a friend,
Right welcome shall he be
To read, to study, not to lend,
But to return to me.
Not that imparted knowledge doth
Diminish learning's store,
But books I find when once they're lent
Return to me no more."

Great collections of books are subject to certain accidents besides the damp, the worms, and the rats; one not less common is that of the *borrowers*, not to say a word of the *purloiners*.

–Isaac D'Israeli

Never lend books, for no one ever returns them; the only books I have in my library are books that other folk have lent me.

–Anatole France

Ever'thing comes t' him who waits but a loaned book.
–Frank McKinney

Borrowing Books

Charles Haddon Spurgeon

But if you feel you must have more books, I recommend to you a little judicious borrowing. You will most likely have some friends who have books, and who will be kind enough to let you use them for a time; and I specially advise you, in order to borrow again, to return whatsoever is lent, promptly, and in good condition. I hope there is not so much need that I should say much about returning books, as there would have been a few months ago, for I have lately met with a statement by a clergyman, which has very much raised my opinion of human nature; for he declares that he has a personal acquaintance with three gentlemen who have actually returned borrowed umbrellas! I am sorry to say that he moves in a more favoured circle than I do, for I have personal acquaintance with several young men who have borrowed books and never returned them. The other day a certain minister, who had lent me five books, which I have used for two years or more, wrote to me a note to request the return of three of them. To his surprise, he had them back by the next "Parcels' Delivery," and two others which he had forgotten. I had carefully kept a list of books borrowed, and, therefore, could make a complete return to the owner. I am sure he did not expect their prompt arrival, for he wrote me a letter of mingled astonishment and gratitude, and when I visit his study again, I feel sure I shall be welcome to another loan.

Thoughts about Books

There is a great deal of difference between the eager man who wants to read a book and the tired man who wants a book to read.

–G. K. Chesterton

Next to acquiring good friends, the best acquisition is that of good books.

–Colton

A man who buys a book is not just buying a few ounces of paper, glue and printer's ink; he may be buying a whole new life.

–Emerson

Some books are to be tasted, others to be swallowed, and some few to be chewed and digested.

–Bacon

Finishing a good book is like leaving a good friend.

–William Feather

The Value of Books

We hear a great deal about the increased cost of living, but never in history could poor people get so much of the life essentials, and even the things that were luxuries a short time ago, for so little money, as today. The products of the greatest minds that have ever lived, were never so cheap. Copies of the great masterpieces of literature, which a century ago were only within the reach of the rich, are now often found in the poorest homes. The printing press has brought the greatest literary wealth within the reach of the poorest people.

How many men and women there are, who think their lives have been failures; who feel dejected, lonely, and shut out from society, and pity themselves because they have not been able to see the world, or mix with people who have done things worth while! Little do these realize that they have right in their own homes, or can easily obtain for a small sum of money, the most precious, the richest sort of friends, guests who would have been more than welcome in the palaces of princes!

Why mourn because your poverty, your lack of chance in life, cuts you off from the society of those who have been more fortunate, when without the exertion of changing your clothing for a social function, you can spend the evening with the kings and queens of the earth, the greatest characters; can without embarrassment or timidity hold communion with the greatest minds that have ever lived!

–Dr. Orison S. Marden

What Do You Think?

The road to ignorance is paved with good editions.
–George Bernard Shaw

Learning hath gained most by those books by which the printers have lost.
–Thomas Fuller

Every man with a bellyfull of classics is an enemy of the human race.
–Henry Miller

It is astonishing how many books I find there is no need for me to read at all.
–W. Somerset Maugham

I wonder whether what we are publishing now is worth cutting down trees to make paper for the stuff.
–Richard Brautigan

Books are fatal; they are the curse of the human race. Nine-tenths of existing books are nonsense, and the clever books are the refutation of that nonsense.
–Benjamin Disraeli

Strong Advice

Oswald Chambers

My strong advice to you is to soak, soak, soak in philosophy and psychology until you know more of these subjects than ever you need consciously to think. It is ignorance of these subjects on the part of ministers and workers that has brought our evangelical theology to such a sorry plight. When people refer to a man as a "man of one book," meaning the Bible, he is generally found to be a man of multitudinous books, which simply isolates the one Book to its proper grandeur. The man who reads only the Bible does not, as a rule, know it or human life.

Library

Ralph Waldo Emerson

Consider what you have in the smallest chosen library. A company of the wisest and wittiest men that could be picked out of all civil countries, in a thousand years, have set in best order the results of their learning and wisdom. The men themselves were hid and inaccessible, solitary, impatient of interruption, fenced by etiquette; but the thought which they did not uncover to their bosom friend is here written out in transparent words to us, the strangers of another age.

Apostle Paul and Books

When Paul's admonition centers in the duty of the minister to know and interpret revelation, it is not to be so construed as to preclude or prohibit the perusal of other volumes. Let us not forget that he who addressed Timothy was himself a scholar. Not only does he quote, in his famous speech on Mars Hill, the Greek poets, Cleanthes and Aratus, but, as Dr. Lightfoot has shown at length and with considerable ingenuity, evinces familiar acquaintance with the teachings of his contemporary, Seneca the Stoic.

Paul assures us that "the God who made the world and all things therein . . . dwelleth not in temples made with hands," and Seneca writes: "Temples must not be built to God of stones piled on high: he must be consecrated in the heart of 'man.'" Moreover, the apostle declares that God is "not far from every one of us"; while the philosopher says, "God is near thee; he is with thee; he is within." Other parallels might be noted, but these are sufficient for our purpose.

Thoughts about Books

It is chiefly through books that we enjoy intercourse with superior minds, and these invaluable means of communication are in the reach of all. In the best books, great men talk to us, give us their most precious thoughts, and pour their souls into ours.

–William E. Channing

My books are friends that never fail me.

–Thomas Carlyle

That place that does contain
My books, the best companions, is to me
A glorious court, where hourly I converse
With the old sages and philosophers;
And sometimes, for variety, I confer
With kings and emperors, and weigh their counsels.

–Francis Beaumont and John Fletcher

A book is the only place in which you can examine a fragile thought without breaking it, or explore an explosive idea without fear it will go off in your face . . . It is one of the few havens remaining where a man's mind can get both provocation and privacy.

–Edward P. Morgan

A Book I'd Like To Share

Actors, Actresses & Comedians

Love Is Eternal

by Irving Stone
Recommended by: Morey Amsterdam

One of my all-time favorite books is *Love Is Eternal.* I happen to be an Abraham Lincoln fan and evidently the research on this book was fantastic. It is the love story of Abraham Lincoln and his wife. When I put it down after reading it, I said to myself, "I knew that man."

Five Minutes to Midnight

by Steve Shagan
Recommended by: Jack Carter

The Secret in the Daisy

by Carol Grace
Recommended by: Walter Matthau

The book that made the greatest difference in my life was *The Secret in the Daisy* by Carol Grace, published in 1955.

The difference it made was enormous. It took me from a miserable unhappy wretch to a joyful, glad-to-be-alive human. I fell so in love with the book that I searched out and married the girl who wrote it.

Mark Twain and the Bible

Recommended by: Bill Cosby

Cosby credits his own mother, Anna, for keeping him from drug abuse and gang fighting as a poor, inner-city youth in Philadelphia. He remembers her reading to him from the Bible and Mark Twain, and says that he never wanted to disappoint her.

Actors, Actresses & Comedians

Peak Performance

by David Krause
Recommended by: Eddie Albert

The Little Prince

by Antoine De Saint-Exupery
Recommended by: Robert Wagner, Actor

One of my favorite books is *The Little Prince*.

"All men have the stars," he answered, "but they are not the same things for different people. For some, who are travelers, the stars are guides. For others they are more than little lights in the sky. For others, who are scholars, they are problems. For businessmen they were wealth. But all these stars are silent. You – you alone – will have the stars as no one else has them –."

"Then you shall judge yourself," the king answered. "That is the most difficult thing of all. It is much more difficult to judge oneself than to judge others. If you succeed in judging yourself rightly, then you are indeed a man of true wisdom."

Other Voices, Other Rooms

by Truman Capote
Recommended by: Jill St. John

Actors & Comedians

The Uses of Adversity

by William Thackeray
Recommended by: Red Skelton

Look Homeward, Angel

by Thomas Wolfe
Recommended by: Tony Randall

When I first read it, I knew very well I wanted to be an actor. There was not the slightest doubt in my mind. I had set my course. By the time I grew out of it, I was an actor.

Anna Karenina

by Leo Tolstoy
Recommended by: Hurd Hatfield

A few years ago a friend asked me if I had read *Anna Karenina* and insisted that I do so. It was a fascinating experience. She had a great understanding of human psychology, the degradation and passion that destroy humanity.

Actors & Comedians

Freedom Road

by Howard Fast
Recommended by: Red Buttons

The Congressional Record

Recommended by: Alan Alda

For some reason, leather bound copies of the goings-on in Congress lined the shelves of our living room, and I pored over them when I was twelve. I had never read anything so funny. From then on, I knew I wanted to do comedy.

A Confederacy of Dunces

by John Kennedy Toole
Recommended by: Mark Russell, Columnist-Comedian

The funniest book I ever read was *A Confederacy of Dunces*, but it also has a sad side. John Kennedy Toole committed suicide at age thirty-two in 1969 before his manuscript was accepted. His mother was so determined to have the work published that she persisted through each rejection until she found a publisher. It became a great hit and received the Pulitzer Award. This book made me both laugh and cry.

The Influence of Books

Golda Meir

"There are evenings in which most of the discussion was about Yiddish literature – Sholom Aleichem, I. L. Peretz, Mendele Mocher Sforim – and other evenings that were devoted to specific questions such as women's suffrage or the future of trade unionism. I was interested in all of it.

"When Morris and I came to know each other better, we started to go to free concerts in the park together, and Morris patiently introduced me to the joys of classical music, read Byron, Shelley, Keats and Rubaiyat of Omar Khayyam to me and took me to lectures on literature, history and philosophy.

"The only place I could read without bothering them – or be disturbed myself by their nightlong coughing – was the bathroom, where wrapped up in a blanket and armed with Morris' current reading list (which was always terrifyingly long) and a pile of books, I used to spend most of my nights."

Aleksandr Solzhenitsyn

The interests of these people were books, ideas, knowledge, and social concerns. When politics were discussed, it was usually in little huddles with nervous glances at the children: will they understand? repeat? give away their parents, even inadvertently? But otherwise – until the blood purges of the 1930s – the atmosphere Aleksandr absorbed was of books and conversations about them.

As his relatives put it, however, Solzhenitsyn was a "boy-intellectual" with a tendency not simply to memorize or study but to "understand the cause of things."

The Influence of Books

Martin Luther King, Jr.

When he entered Morehouse College at the age of fifteen, he expected to be a doctor. A year or so later, his ambition switched to law. Not until the summer of his junior year, when he worked (once again from choice, not necessity) in the tobacco fields of Conn., did he realize that his calling had to be the ministry. Already the teachings of Mahatma Gandhi had begun to shape his thinking. He was intrigued and enthralled by Thoreau, the quiet philosopher of Walden. Later, when he studied theology at Crozer Seminary in Chester, Penna., and received his Ph.D. from Boston University and his Doctor of Divinity degree from Chicago Theological Seminary, he found a special appeal to the works of the Biblical prophets Amos, Isaiah, Jeremiah and Micah, "for their emphasis was not on ceremonial but on social justice in religion."

Frederick Douglas

"Filled with the determination to learn to read at any cost, I hit upon many expedients to accomplish that much desired end. The plan which I mainly adopted, and the one which was the most successful, was that of using my young white playmates, with whom I met on the streets, as teachers. I used to carry almost constantly a copy of Webster's spelling-book in my pocket, and when sent on errands, or when play-time was allowed me, I would step aside with my young friends and take a lesson in spelling. I am greatly indebted to these boys – Gustavus Dorgan, Joseph Bailey, Charles Farity, and William Cosdry."

How to Get Control of Your Time and Your Life

by Alan Lakein
Recommended by: W. E. Adamson, President, Rich-United Corp.

I have chosen *How To Get Control of Your Time and Your Life* by Alan Lakein. This book was written at a very important time for my life.

I was thirty-one years old, fairly successful in individual sales, but totally disorganized and losing my goal orientation. By reading this book, Mr. Lakein inspired me to determine a dramatic and awesome responsibility, which was to set lifetime goals. The awesomeness of that seemed too much to handle, but through a step-by-step process and by a theory of arranging goals in categories, and also by recognizing that lifetime goals at thirty-one were not necessarily the lifetime goals at fifty-one, I was able to truly sit down and do some long-range goal setting. The contents of this book allowed me to multiply my meager holdings ten-fold in less than ten years.

In perusing this book, I feel it is more up-to-date in 1984 than it was when it was published, and I would recommend it highly.

Horatio Alger and Moby Dick

"Am reading *Moby Dick* and find it exciting. What a thrilling life the literary must be! Imagination and observation – these I take to be the important requisites. Would it be desirable for me to take up writing as a life work? The satisfaction resulting from a beautiful story must be inspiring – a story that rouses readers to a new sense of the fine things of life. Have I the ability to write? Why not – if I am conscientious and observe closely all that goes on about me?"

By the time he was eight, Alger was a living monument to his father's zealous purpose. He was knowledgeable in American history and geography, a formidable speller, an able mathematician, conversant with Plato, fluent in Latin, thoroughly familiar with the Bible.

Horatio was already familiar with everything the Bible had to say. He could not help it because he was compelled to sit quietly and attentively beside his father to watch Pastor Alger write his lengthy sermons and when they were done, the minister read them back to his captive audience, requiring the boy to write down a synopsis of each one after he had heard it.

Presidents

The White-Boned Demon

by Ross Terrill
Recommended by: Philip H. Knight,
President, Nike, Inc.

A book which I have profited from is *The White-Boned Demon*. This is a biography of Madame Mao Zedong. The reason this book has had the impact it has, is that it brings to light the fact that people in other countries think so differently from us.

How to Improve Your Serve

by Chuck Swindoll
Recommended by: W. R. Lundquist,
President, Homes & Lands Publishing Corp.

Money Market Book

by Marsha Stigum
Recommended by: Deborah S. McGuire,
President, First Woman's Bank of Maryland

This book is excellent for the individual who has no understanding of the financial money markets and how they operate. Mrs. Stigum very clearly defines how the banking system works and how all of the financial products are traded in the marketplace. She covers all of the money market instruments, such as Certificates of Deposit, EuroDollar Deposits, Bankers Acceptances, Treasury Bills, Notes and Bonds, Agency Issues and many other aspects of the financial money markets. I highly recommend this book to financial professionals who feel that this area is foreign to their knowledge.

This is one of the books which has benefited me most in recent times.

Presidents

Magic of Believing

by Claude Bristol
Recommended by: John Bontreger
President, Signature Inns

Seeds of Greatness

by Denis Waitley
Recommended by: Jackie Cooper,
President, Jackie B. Cooper & Associates

Love Is Letting Go of Fear

by Gerald Jampolsky
Recommended by: Pam Lontos,
President, Pam Lontos, Inc.

The Little Engine that Could

by Watty Piper
Recommended by: Don Dible, President,
Dible Management Development Institute, Inc.

Enthusiasm Makes the Difference

by Norman Vincent Peale
Recommended by: Ed Street,
President, Street Construction

The Influence of Books

Dag Hammarskjöld – Buber and à Kempis

The Swedish publishers whom Hammarskjöld approached with the proposal of translating *I and Thou* were enthusiastic about it, and he decided to begin work on the project. He left New York for Africa on September 12. He took two books with him: Thomas à Kempis's *Imitation of Christ* and *I and Thou*. While in Leopoldville in the Congo attempting to resolve a civil war, he apparently worked on the translation. On September 17 he flew to Northern Rhodesia, leaving behind in his room, to which he expected to return after his trip, the first twelve pages of his translation of *I and Thou*. He had made some handwritten corrections on the first page.

His plane never reached its destination. It crashed in the jungle, killing everyone aboard.

Stephen M. Panko

Charles George Gordon and à Kempis

"Gordon of Khartoum"

Power wrote to his mother on February 22, "Gordon is a most lovable character – quiet, mild, gentle, and strong; he is so humble too. The way he pats you on the shoulder when he says, 'Look here, dear fellow, now what would you advise?' would make you love him. . . . It is wonderful that one man could have such an influence on 200,000 people. Numbers of women flock here every day to ask him to touch their children to cure them; they call him the 'Father and the Saviour of the Sudan.' He has found me badly up in *Thomas à Kempis*, which he reads every day, and has given me an *Imitation of Christ*. He is indeed, I believe, the greatest and best man of this century."

The Influence of Books

Martin Buber and Education

There was a strong emphasis on Jewish tradition in the home, but along with the study of the Bible and the Talmud, there was an emphasis on European languages. Solomon and Adela Buber were a new kind of learned Jew; they felt as comfortable studying Goethe and Schiller and other German authors as they were with the Torah and the Midrash. Their grandson was exposed to the same mixture of classical Jewish and non-Jewish writings. He did not go to school until he was ten years of age, but was taught privately at home.

His grandparents were a great influence in his life. His grandfather took him for long walks so that he might learn to love nature as well as books.

Anwar Sadat and Books

"Apart from the political activities in which I was immersed as soon as I graduated from the academy, I committed myself to cultural pursuits, which I felt were equally important inasmuch as they supported my political activity. That was why I tried to join the British Institute in Egypt and obtain a B.A. from the University of London. I was also very fond of reading. While in Cairo, I got my books from second-hand bookshops around Izbekih Park; in the provinces I wrote to the publishers and bookstores for book lists. Whatever I picked was sent direct to Second Lieutenant Muhammad Anwar el-Sadat, wherever I was stationed."

"It was perhaps this that particularly distinguished me from my colleagues. When in Manqabad, I remember, a special army bus used to take us every Thursday afternoon to Asyut, where we spent the whole evening. My colleagues went to the movies or sought other entertainments. I sat at a cafe near the railway station, smoked a hookah, and happily read the books I had bought in Cairo, until my colleagues were ready to return and we all took the bus back to camp."

Presidents

Something for Joey

by Richard Peck

Gifford on Courage

by Frank Gifford
Recommended by: Michael Aun, II, CSP,
President, Aun & Associates

I would suggest two of my favorite inspirational books that I pull out from time to time when I'm a bit down and out.

Something for Joey is a book that will make you cry from the minute you open the front cover. It is a heart-warming true story about the courage and love between Heisman Trophy football standout John Cappelletti and his baby brother Joey, who died of leukemia.

The second book is *Gifford on Courage*, by Frank Gifford with Charles Mangel. Sportscaster and former athlete Frank Gifford shares the real life stories of ten great athletes who overcame various obstacles to succeed in sports. They are Herb Score, Rocky Bleier, Charley Boswell, Don Klosterman, Floyd Layne, Charlie Conerly, Y. A. Tittle, Dan Gable, Willis Reed and Ken Venturi. His book will make you laugh and cry as you watch these men overcome impossible hurdles to go on to victory.

See You at the Top

by Zig Ziglar
Recommended by: Mike Frank
President, Speakers Unlimited

How to Motivate Other People

by L. K. Roberts
Recommended by: Andre De LaRonde
President, HAD Inc., Canada

Professionals

A Man for All Seasons

by Robert Bolt
Recommended by: William B. Ball,
Constitutional Lawyer, Harrisburg, Pa.

The books I have read which have been of deep importance in my life . . . At the top of the list would have to be the New Testament. Everything else would have to be secondary. Among great "secondaries" are Robert Bolt's great play, *A Man For All Seasons*, much of Shakespeare, and Russell Kirk's *The Roots of American Order*.

Don't Choke: How Athletes Can Become Winners

by M. Scott & L. Pelliccioni, Jr.
Recommended by: Dr. Sam Gamber
Dillsburg, Pa.

Theory Z—How American Business Can Meet the Japanese Challenge

by William G. Ouchi
Recommended by: Raymon J. Baker, Consultant
Management Advisory Group, Inc.

Two books immediately come to mind which have had an impact upon me. The first is *Theory Z—How American Business Can Meet the Japanese Challenge*, written by a Japanese-American, William Ouchi. I found this book to be very enlightening. The same can be said about *Quality Is Free*, which was written by Philip Crosby while he served as a Corporate Vice President of ITT and was responsible for quality operations worldwide. This latter book confirms a conviction of mine that a quality product can be produced more cheaply than a mediocre one, particularly when the long view is considered.

The Success System that Never Fails

by W. Clement Stone
Recommended by: Paul Barber,
Exec. Vice-President, Junior Achievement

Is there a guaranteed formula for success? According to W. Clement Stone, "Gifted men were made, not born"; therefore, almost anyone can improve and become "gifted."

The procedure was this. Just before going to sleep at kind of stories that inspire. Principles are related by "italicizing" them. The three necessary ingredients for success which are expanded upon are:

"1. *Inspiration to Action:* That which motivates you to act because you WANT to.

"2. *Know How:* The particular techniques and skill that consistently get results for you. KNOW HOW is the proper application of knowledge. KNOW HOW becomes habit through actual repetitive experience.

"3. *Activity Knowledge:* Knowledge of the activity, service, product, methods, techniques, and skills with which you are particularly concerned."

He'll share how, "FAILURE IS GOOD FOR YOU IF YOU LEARN FROM IT," and explain such statements as, "YOU'VE GOT A PROBLEM?–THAT'S GOOD!"

It is a virtual encyclopedia of principles which makes it worthy not only to read, but to study as you would a textbook. For easy reference, each chapter has a summary called "Little Hinges that Swing Big Doors."

Professional Athletes

Loving God

by Charles Colson
Recommended by: Steve Bartkowski,
Football Player, Atlanta Falcons

My choice of the book that has been the most influential to me is *Loving God*. The author is a great communicator of spiritual principles. His book is alive and exciting in the way Chuck Colson uses true-life personalities and situations to develop his theme. The book shows clearly how we can better improve our lives by more completely teaching us how to love our God.

Strengthening Your Grip

by Charles Swindoll
Recommended by: Augie Ruiz
Baseball Player, Atlanta Braves

My all-time favorite book for reading is of course the Bible, but another book that has given me blessings is *Strengthening Your Grip*. Charles Swindoll has truly been a teacher and inspiration with all the books that he has written.

Iacocca, an Autobiography

by Lee Iacocca and William Novak
Recommended by: Jay Carroll,
Football Player, Tampa Bay Buccaneers

This book opened my eyes to the world of big business. It also showed me the type of character it takes to be a great leader.

Grinding It Out: The Making of McDonald's

by Ray Kroc
Recommended by: Frank Basile, Certified Speaking Professional

They called Ray Kroc, the founder of McDonald's, "Danny Daydreamer" in school because of the schemes he thought up. Well, he never stopped daydreaming until his death in early 1984.

Even after the company was a phenomenal success and he had pioneered so many aspects of the fast food industry and business in general, he continued to daydream. He set up such things as philanthropic organizations to aid all kinds of good causes and continued to pioneer new industry breakthroughs which have now become legend.

But, as he noted throughout his book, the key to this success was not his daydreaming, although it was a necessary prelude to that success. The key, as indicated in the title of the book, was the fact that he was always grinding it out. Every day, day in and day out, he did the things necessary to succeed even though he had many, many interim setbacks and even though at many times everything looked dismal. Success, he pointed out, does not come overnight but as a result of constant, daily application and work.

Another supporting theme which ran through Ray Kroc's book was his constant thirst for knowledge and then his application of that knowledge. He concluded his book by saying, "At the age of 75, McDonald's and I are both still green and growing." Yes, Ray Kroc was still grinding it out when he wrote his book in 1976 and when he died at a young 83 in 1984.

The Greatest Miracle in the World

by Og Mandino
Recommended by: Dennis Beecher, President, Amdeka Corporation

The books I've listed below have all been extremely motivating in assisting my wife and me to a balanced life and success in all we attempt.

1. *The Greatest Miracle in the World*

2. *The Greatest Secret in the World*

3. *The Greatest Salesman in the World*

4. *Life is Tremendous*. This one has not only created our leadership traits but its author's life proves its worth. The second paragraph on page 102 is the real key to all success!

"A cardinal rule to remember in reading inspirational books: You only get to keep and enjoy what you share and give away. If you aren't going to read with the purpose of sharing and giving, I suggest you give the books to someone who will share with you and you'll discover the power of books as you watch the reader grow through sharing with you. Perhaps the best idea would be to use the 'brain trust' idea of 'Think and Grow Rich' and both of you begin reading and sharing with each other."

I Can

by Ben Sweetland
Recommended by: Vicki Bennett,
President, Bennett Productions, Australia

When I was at the impressionable age of fifteen, my father invested in a book for me which helped shape my future in going on to become the first female saleswoman of the Xerox Corporation in Australia, and then to becoming a speaker and author in my own right.

Ben Sweetland first brought my attention to the power of the mind and how to develop the "CONSCIOUS AND CREATIVE MIND."

He says that "you learned that thoughts maintained in your CONSCIOUS MIND are accepted as instruction by your CREATIVE MIND which acts accordingly.

"In this chapter you are learning that you think in terms of pictures not words. This will enable you to understand that your mental pictures are PATTERNS, which are acted upon by your CREATIVE MIND.

"The dominant thought being developed now is: You are AS you are due to the type of thoughts you have been thinking up to this point. What you will be in weeks, months and years to come WILL DEPEND ON THE THOUGHTS you will hold FROM THIS POINT ONWARD. This last sentence will be encouraging to you, because it means that, if you are not satisfied with yourself as you are at this moment, you have within your being the POWER to change yourself or any given situation by changing your THOUGHTS, or as you now understand it, creating new mental PICTURE PATTERNS."

This technique has and will continue to enable me to shape my own destiny. Thank you, Ben Sweetland.

Professional Speakers

Becoming Your Best Self

Recommended by: Mort Utley, CPAE

The Aerobics Program for Total Well-Being

by Dr. Kenneth Cooper
Recommended by: Ed Foreman, CPAE

Tough Times Never Last but Tough People Do

by Dr. Robert H. Schuller
Recommended by: Joan Jewett, Certified Speaking Professional

How to Win Friends and Influence People

by Dale Carnegie
Recommended by: Les Giblin Certified Speaking Professional

Art of Understanding Yourself

by Cecil Osborne
Recommended by: Mary Ellen Coburn, Certified Speaking Professional, President, Image Consultants

Authors on Biographies

Frank Bettger
How I Raised Myself from Failure to Success in Selling

Many years later, when I was groping around in the dark, desperately trying to learn how to sell, I picked up a book that had a tremendous effect on my life, *The Autobiography of Benjamin Franklin*.

He thought of himself as a simple man of ordinary ability, but believed he could acquire the essential principles of successful living, if only he could find the right method. Having an inventive mind, he devised a method so simple, yet so practical, that anyone could use it.

When I first read these words, I turned back eagerly to the page where Franklin began to explain his plan. Over the years, I have re-read those pages dozens of times. It was like a legacy to me!

Remember Franklin was a scientist. This plan is scientific. Reject it, and you reject one of the most practical ideas ever offered you. I know. I know what it did for me. I know it can do the same for anyone who will try it. It's not an easy way. There is no easy way. But it is a sure way.

Franklin's Thirteen Subjects

Temperance – Silence – Order – Resolution
Frugality – Industry – Sincerity – Justice
Moderation – Cleanliness – Tranquility
Chastity – Humility

Authors on Biographies

Napoleon Hill

"Long before I had ever written a line for publication, or endeavored to deliver a speech in public, I followed the habit of reshaping my own character, by trying to imitate the nine men whose lives and lifeworks had been most impressive to me.

"These nine men were Emerson, Paine, Edison, Darwin, Lincoln, Burbank, Napoleon, Ford, and Carnegie. Every night, over a long period of years, I held an imaginary council meeting with this group whom I called my 'Invisible Counselors.'

The procedure was this. Just before going to sleep at night, I would shut my eyes, and see, in my imagination, this group of men seated with me around my council table. Here I had not only an opportunity to sit among those whom I considered to be great, but I actually dominated the group by serving as chairman."

Zig Ziglar

"Regularly read Horatio Alger stories. Read the biographies and the autobiographies of the men and women of every race, creed and color who used what they had and got a great deal out of life by making contributions to life. It would be difficult, if not impossible, to read the life stories of Henry Ford, Carneigie, Booker T. Washington, etc., and not be inspired. I challenge anybody to read the story of Eartha White, daughter of an ex-slave, which appeared in the December 1974 issue of *Reader's Digest*, and not be inspired to do more with their life. We relate to these stories and when we see them succeeding, we visualize ourselves doing the same thing."

Psycho-Cybernetics

by Dr. Maxwell Maltz
Recommended by: James "Doc" Blakely, Ph.D., CPAE, Certified Speaking Professional

Psycho-Cybernetics was the turning point for me in realizing my full potential as a professional humorist. The title itself means "steersman." The philosophy of the book is that we can chart a path for our mind to travel and it is up to us to take the helm with confidence and reach our destination by setting goals.

Dr. Maltz, now deceased, was a plastic surgeon. He found that some people did not need plastic surgery on their face or body, but rather mental surgery on their mind. Like the story of the woman who had had her face lifted so many times that her toes curled, we tend to laugh at anyone who cosmetically covers up a defect.

For men, one insecurity is baldness. Everyone loves the joke about the guy who is going through the buffet line, a plate in each hand, leans over to take a closer look, and his hairpiece falls in the cheese dip. "Everyone knows who did it. He is the only one with padded shoulders, taller-than-she-is shoes, pancake make-up, and a gorgeous suntan except for the top of his head which is as white as a gourd."

Believe it or not, *Psycho-Cybernetics* taught me how to live with my own imperfections and joke about those of others who also often recognize that people love them just the way they are.

Woman of Valor

by Irving Fineman
Recommended by: Veachey R. Bloom,
President, Samard Enterprises

The book that has made a lasting impression on me is *Woman of Valor*, by Irving Fineman, which chronicles the life of Henrietta Szold, 1860–1945.

She rose from a daughter of Baltimore to "mother" of thousands of children whom she spirited from death at the hands of Hitler – to life in the Holy Land.

She wrote that "biography should be more than chronicle. It should stimulate thought, influence action, lead to introspection and creation." Her biography and the example of her life have done those things for the hundreds of thousands of American Women who belong to the organization she founded in 1912 dedicated to education, medicine, and rehabilitation.

She spoke as a woman, urging other women to rise up for "noble discontent," and she told her feelings as a woman. Her daring courage, and her gigantic achievements are attributed to a magnificent personality. In her life, she experienced loss, frustration, and sorrow; but she persisted to try to right the wrongs of the world as she perceived them, and to build for the future of mankind.

She has become eternal. She was truly a woman of valor, who "excellest them all."

Bunkhouse Logic

by Ben Stein
Recommended by: Ty Boyd, CPAE,
Past President, National Speakers Association

I try to read a book a week. Internalizing the experiences and skills of others allows me to broaden my horizons.

Bunkhouse Logic knocked my socks off. Ben Stein says it succinctly: "I must take *responsibility* for me. *My* actions determine my rewards. Ain't nobody gonna ride a white charger up the stairs, down the hall, past the secretary, to my little cubicle and say 'I'm here to deliver you into the hands of achievement.'"

If it is to be, it is up to me. Ben Stein got to me like mainlining gets to a junkie.

"YOU CAN'T WIN IF YOU'RE NOT AT THE TABLE." That's the obvious, but overlooked, requisite in the game of success. But Stein also discusses 10 Rules of the game that give good directions for your "next steps," once the decision to get to the table is made.

I can't remember ever finding as many valuable insights in one small volume!

"The logic of the bunkhouse requires constant activity, incessant mobility, emphasis on performance, not excuses. All of this corresponds to an astonishing extent with the practices of the successful."

"When you study these rules of *Bunkhouse Logic* think of the American cowboy. Day after day he bets on himself to win. He always collects the money. You will have a better idea of what the rules are about if you bear him in mind."

More Than a Carpenter

by Josh McDowell
Recommended by: J. Pat Branch, Rodeo Performer

This is a simple but true book, backed up with pragmatic and historical references:

"Will Durant, who was trained in the discipline of historical investigation and spent his life analyzing records of antiquity, writes: 'Despite the prejudices and theological preconceptions of the evangelists, they record many incidents that mere inventors would have concealed – the competition of the apostles for high places in the Kingdom, their flight after Jesus' arrest, Peter's denial, the failure of Christ to work miracles in Galilee, the references of some auditors to his possible insanity, his early uncertainty as to his mission, his confessions of ignorance as to the future, his moments of bitterness, his despairing cry on the cross; no one reading those scenes can doubt the reality of the figure behind them. That a few simple men should in one generation have invented so powerful and appealing a personality, so lofty an ethic, and so inspiring a vision of human brotherhood, would be a miracle far more incredible than any recorded in the Gospels. After two centuries of Higher Criticism the outlines of the life, character, and teaching of Christ remain reasonably clear, and constitute the most fascinating feature in the history of Western man.'"

Professional Speakers

How I Raised Myself from Failure to Success In Selling

by Frank Bettger
Recommended by: Newt Hielscher, CPAE

See You at the Top

by Zig Ziglar
Recommended by: Bob Sweeney
Certified Speaking Professional, England

How to Make Yourself Miserable

by Dan Greenburg
Recommended by: Frank Swiatek,
Certified Speaking Professional

Gift from the Sea

by Anne M. Lindbergh
Recommended by: Rosita Perez, Certified
Speaking Professional, Creative Living Programs

Tony, the Bricklayer

Recommended by: Joyce Turley,
Certified Speaking Professional

Professional Speakers

Mornings on Horseback

by David McCullough
Recommended by: Michael Broome

I suppose my favorite, in recent years, would be *Mornings On Horseback*, by David McCullough.

It is a fascinating account of Teddy Roosevelt's parents, their influence upon him and his growth to young manhood. It presents an inspiring account of one family who truly lived their ideals and possessed a zest for living.

Since the only families that get attention today are either in the midst of murder or divorce trials, or feuding on some godless prime time series, it was a pleasure to read how love, not money, power and sex, was at the center of this family's relationship.

The Master Game

by Robert DeRopp
Recommended by: Ross V. Hersey

The Master Game, by Robert DeRopp, is a fantastic book that combines some Zen philosophy with some practical, down-to-earth common sense we all need.

It says that man's ordinary state of consciousness, his so-called waking state, is not the highest level of consciousness of which he is capable. *The Master Game* seeks to elevate us to a higher level of understanding, to find the true awakening and full development of the powers latent in man.

It says, "The good effort of each man, benefits all men, the error or evil of each man augments the tribulation of all men. As moves the part, so moves the whole. As the progress of the whole, so the progress of the part. I am a part, you are a part, and each of us advances or retards the whole by how we be."

Babbitt

by Sinclair Lewis
Recommended by: Earl Brodie,
Certified Speaking Professional

One of my favorite books is probably *Babbitt*, by the late Sinclair Lewis. It was written in 1922 and has always been considered a rather bitter satire on American businessmen in the just-make-a-living sector of the economy. He was, to a large degree, right, but he did give us hope.

I'm going to quote from the last page of *Babbitt*. Babbit's son, Ted, has refused to go to the University, has married his girl friend, although both are still under 20 years of age, and he wants to take a job doing mechanical work in a factory. This disappoints the Babbitt family, with all their college degrees and middle class white collar values. Babbitt speaks:

". . . I've never done a single thing I've wanted to do in my whole life. I don't know that I've accomplished anything except just get along. I figure out I've made about a quarter of an inch out of a possible hundred rods . . . maybe you'll carry things on further . . . those folks in there will try to bully you, and tame you down. Tell them to go to the devil! I'll back you. Take your factory job if you want to. Don't be scared of the family, no, nor all of Zenith. Nor of yourself, the way I've been. Go ahead old man! The world is yours!"

I suspect that the thing that separates the men from the boys in this world is that we've been able to empathize with Babbittry without becoming Babbitts.

Monday Morning Christianity

by Dr. Harry Olson
Recommended by: Eugene Broecker, CLU,
Insurance Marketing Institute, Purdue Univ.

The primary reason that I have such an admiration for Dr. Harry Olson's book *Monday Morning Christianity* is that back in the mid 70s when I was asked to be the Director of the Insurance Marketing Institute, I was concerned about the responsibilities of the new position and, frankly, although it was a great honor, I was not sure if I could handle it.

Ironically, at that time I had not met Harry Olson, but had asked him to speak at a conference here at Purdue University. His book had "just hit the streets" and he gave me a copy. I started reading a chapter each morning as soon as I hit the office. Although life still has its ups and downs, the "battery charging" I get from Harry's book is almost unbelievable.

One of my favorite chapters in his book is called "One More Time." After reading about the "mumpsimus" syndrome, which is "a persistent belief in a mistaken idea," I've come to the realization that if we continue to believe in past and mistaken ideas, we are surely in trouble. It has changed my thinking tremendously.

Tom Landry, who did the foreword in the book, sums it up when he says, "We attend the church of our choice on Sunday, but never really get into the game. On Monday our lives do not reflect what we profess to be."

Window of Opportunity

by Newt Gingrich
Recommended by: David Anderson Brown, Vice-Pres., Life Management Services

There are two classic forces fighting each other within the United States: One is the entrepreneurial spirit which creates unlimited opportunities for challenging careers and jobs for working America. The other force, known as "Big Government," has developed into a freewheeling system that rewards individuals for non-productive behavior as it doles out the hard-earned dollars of the taxpayer. Over the past couple decades, the line has been clearly drawn: businessman vs. bureaucrat, with the politician, who once served as referee, now serving as player-coach on the Bureaucratic team.

In *Window of Opportunity*, Georgia Congressman Newt Gingrich brings a welcome vision of possible relief to this counterproductive drain of energy. Speaking the entrepreneur's language, he describes the "Opportunity Society" America's hope for the future:

"The opportunity society understands the enormous power which dreams have on people . . . it is clear that human beings will take great risks and endure extreme privations if their dream is large enough.

"We must encourage the production of new wealth, new ideas, and new inventions, as we must bias our society in favor of entrepreneurs and hard work."

Gingrich's book left me with a greater sense of meaning and purpose in what I do as a businessman, and with a feeling of hope for the future of America's Free Enterprise System.

Presidents

Arrowsmith

by Sinclair Lewis
Recommended by: Glenn T. Seaborg, Scientist, President, International Platform Society

I would identify *Arrowsmith* as a book that was a source of inspiration to me as a young man. This absorbing and dramatic description of a struggling young scientist and his personal rewards did much to increase my resolve to pursue science as a career.

Ten Days to a Great New Life

by William E. Edwards
Recommended by: Wayne Pribble, President, Pribble Enterprises, Inc.

In Search of Excellence

by Thomas Peters and Robert Waterman, Jr.
Recommended by: Richard P. Shelly, President, Harrisburg Area YMCA

Down the Proverb Path

by Solomon
Recommended by: E. J. Plott, President, Plott Realtors

Tough Times Never Last, but Tough People Do

by Robert H. Schuller
Recommended by: Bob Mohr, President, Mohr & Associates

Freedom of Simplicity

by Richard J. Foster
Recommended by: Dr. Fred Bryan,
Former President, Mansfield State College

Anyone who is striving to be a child of God should study the contents of a little book, *Freedom of Simplicity*.

I consciously use the expression STUDY THE CONTENTS because it is not the kind of book that should be read and returned to the library shelf. It should be read over and over again until the Good News of the Gospel has taken root in our lives.

According to Foster, Christian simplicity lives in harmony with the ordered complexity of life. And isn't this what Christians are seeking? We must live in two worlds at the same time. We want to live the Good Life and at the same time cope comfortably with the complexities of the material world. According to Foster, Christian simplicity makes this possible.

Foster does not give a simple definition of simplicity. He explains how we receive the grace of simplicity by placing less value on things we possess; by coping with the hard social realities of life; and by seeking the Inner Peace that comes as a gift from God to those who know "The beauty of simplicity in thought, conduct and speech."

Foster writes "forcefully, honestly, and tenderly." His words will change lives. All who are privileged to study his little book, *Freedom of Simplicity*, will be forever indebted to him.

I Dare You

by William H. Danforth
Recommended by: Billy Burden,
Certified Speaking Professional, Author

If you came from a poverty-stricken background and had inferiority complexes coming out your ears as a kid, as I did, you needed someone to DARE YOU. In 1949, that DARE came to me in the form of a book–a book given then and still being given today to many graduating high school seniors.

At a time when I was leaving home for whatever the world had to offer, I needed the I DARE YOU challenge.

In his preface, Mr. Danforth says *I Dare You!* is for the daring few who are headed somewhere. Those afraid to DARE might as well pass it up. It will weary the lazy because it calls for immediate action. It will bore the sophisticated, and amuse the skeptics. It calls for courage, swift and daring.

I read *I Dare You!* As a teenager, it put me on the "right track" and it has had a lasting influence on my life.

After reading Mr. Danforth's book, the words "I DARE YOU" kept ringing in my ears. Through the years, I have attempted things that I would never have attempted if it had not been for a little voice inside me that has continued to whisper "I DARE YOU!" Each time I have failed that same little voice has not whispered, it has yelled, "I DARE YOU to pick yourself up and try again."

Thanks to Mr. Danforth's book, I know that in order to "touch the stars," one must reach beyond.

The Business of Living

by Jack H. Grossman
Recommended by: A. C. Carlson, President, A. C. Carlson Company

Much has been written on how to make a living. It is refreshing to find books written on how to live. After all, we are or should be in the business of living.

Some thoughts and quotes from this book are:

"Most people, if given a choice, would not want to die. Yet so few people choose to live."

"Living means actively taking steps to make the most of yourself, your experiences, and your environment."

"Living is taking advantage of opportunities that can help you develop as a person."

This book covers the value and purpose of living a meaningful life and utilizing your full potential. Other great thoughts the author shares with his readers are that living is the business of making desires and dreams come true; and reflecting on the past is healthy only if it helps you chart the future.

Andrew Carnegie and Books

When I asked Andrew Carnegie what his first wages were, he replied, "One dollar and twenty cents a week was what I received as a bobbin boy in a cotton factory, and I can tell you that I considered it pretty good, at that. When I was thirteen, I had learned to run a steam engine, and for that I received a dollar and eighty cents a week."

"You had no early schooling, then?"

"None, except such as I gave myself. There were no fine libraries then, but in Allegheny City, where I lived, there was a certain Colonel Anderson, who was well to do and of a philanthropic turn. He announced about the time I first began to work, that he would be in his library at his home, every Saturday, ready to lend books to working boys and men. He only had about four hundred volumes, but I doubt if ever so few books were put to better use. Only he who has longed, as I did, for Saturday to come, that the spring of knowledge might be opened anew to him, can understand what Colonel Anderson did for me and the others of the boys of the Allegheny. Quite a number of them have risen to eminence, and I think their rise can easily be traced to this splendid opportunity."

–Dr. Marden

This Is Earl Nightingale

by Earl Nightingale
Recommended by: Nick Carter, CPAE
Vice-President, Nightingale-Conant Corporation

In this book, you will find one hundred of Earl's most requested radio shows from over the years, all embellished nicely with applicable quotes from many of the great minds who have walked this planet Earth since the dawn of civilization.

It's the perfect companion to have by your bedside. The articles are very concise, but each offers one of those life-changing concepts for which Mr. Nightingale is so widely recognized and admired.

Indeed, if you'd allow me only one book to help me develop my life, I sincerely believe this would be my choice!

"You have a rudder-like control on your life, and you get that control largely by the goals you set with deep desire."

"Treat every person you meet like he or she is the most important person on earth and it will help your human relations."

"The picture you have of yourself, your self-esteem, will have a profound effect on the way you see the world and the way your world sees you."

Self Creation

by Dr. George Weinberg
Recommended by: Jim Cathcart, Certified Speaking Professional

The quality of our lives is determined by our own thoughts and actions. Dr. Weinberg shows clearly how we can manage both the thoughts and the actions to "Create" the kind of life we'd like to have.

His approach is very practical with dozens of step-by-step "how to's." The essence of the book is the Self-Creation Principle: "Every time you act, you add strength to the motivating idea behind what you've done."

Readers will especially enjoy finding out how to avoid or overcome depression, build enthusiasm, eradicate fears and increase self-discipline. Look at these chapter titles for some insight into his lighthearted, yet serious style:

Have Yourself a Happy Trauma
How to Be a Paranoid
The Harmful Act of Doing Nothing
How to Deal with Infuriating People

This book is great reference material. Set it on a handy shelf for day-to-day reference. The step-by-step approach in each article tells how to handle each challenge "by the numbers."

May you gain as much from the book as I have. Happy "creating."

Authors on Books

James Baldwin

You think your pain and your heartbreak are unprecedented in the history of the world, but then you read. It was books that taught me that the things that tormented me most were the very things that connected me with all the people who were alive, or who had ever been alive.

Joseph Conrad

Of all the inanimate objects, of all men's creations, books are the nearest to us, for they contain our very thoughts, our ambitions, our indignations, our illusions, our fidelity to truth, and our persistent leaning toward error. But most of all they resemble us in their precarious hold on life.

James Russell Lowell

Have you ever rightly considered what the mere ability to read means? That it is the key which admits us to the whole world of thought and fancy and imagination? To the company of saint and sage, of the wisest and the wittiest at their wisest and wittiest moment? That it enables us to see with the keenest eyes, hear with the finest ears, and listen to the sweetest voices of all time?

Hesse on Books

Leaves of Grass

by Walt Whitman

Whoever reads this book at the right hour will find in it something of the primeval world and something of the high mountains, of the ocean and the prairies. Much will strike him as shrill and almost grotesque, but the work will impress him, just as America impresses us, even if against our will.

Faust

by Goethe

For almost a hundred years now scholars and amateurs have tried their hands at interpreting the second part of Goethe's *Faust* and have found the most beautiful and the most stupid, the profoundest and the most banal interpretations for it. But in every work of poetry, though perhaps hidden, there lurks under the surface that nameless ambiguity, that "overdetermination of symbols," as the newer psychology has it. Without having recognized this, be it only a single time, in all its infinite fullness and inexhaustible significance, you stand handicapped before every poet and thinker, you take for the whole what is a small part, you believe in interpretations that barely touch the surface.

The Catcher In the Rye

by J. D. Salinger

"Whether one reads this novel as the individual story of a half-grown problem child or as the allegory of a whole country and people, one will be led by the author along the beautiful road from dislike to understanding, from disgust to love. In a problematic world and time, poetry can achieve nothing higher."

Bertrand Russel and Boethius

"During the two centuries before his time and the ten centuries after it, I cannot think of any European man of learning so free from superstition and fanaticism. . . . He would have been remarkable in any age; in the age in which he lived, he is utterly amazing.

Boethius lived in Italy in the days when the Roman Empire in the west was disintegrating into a mosaic of barbarian successor-states. At first he served the greatest of the barbarians, Theodoric, but he was eventually imprisoned for political reasons and was executed in 524. His importance lies in the fact that he provided a link between Greek philosophy and the thought of the Dark Ages. For six centuries all that the west knew of Aristotle was the fragment which Boethius had had time to translate. In his own writings Boethius was regarded as a very Christian philosopher, yet the essence of his thought was Platonic rather than specifically Christian."

Eric Hoffer on Von Karman

Von Karman's *The Wind and Beyond* is a delight. I am learning something and also enjoying myself. Good stories. The one I like best is about David Helbert, the great mathematician. At a party in his house, his wife asked him to change his tie. He went up to the bedroom and did not return. When his wife went up to see what had happened to him she found him fast asleep in bed. He had taken off his tie, and since this was normally the first step in undressing he simply continued and went to sleep.

This delightful story reminded me of the predicament of the old: they have the failings and the needs of genius. They are as absent-minded as a great mathematician, and like creative people they need recognition and praise in order to function well.

Von Karman's father thought that the life span of an idea is 150 years (five generations). He predicted that nationalism, which took hold in 1800, would begin to die in 1950.

Of what do ideas die? Some die of excess. The excesses of the religious wars put an end to religiosity just as nationalist excesses are bringing nationalism to an end. Industrialism too seems likely to die of excess. The idea of hope died from expecting too much and taking too much for granted. The hopeful generation that stumbled into the First World War took civilized life for granted. The life span of the idea of hope, from the Encyclopedists to 1914, was about 150 years.

Reading von Karman, one realizes what a potent key mathematics is for the unlocking of nature's secrets. One is also aware that, in aerodynamics as in man's soul, the trivial is not trivial. A slight change in design can have momentous consequences.

Authors

Eric Hoffer and History

I am reading Yevgenia Ginzburg's *Journey into the Whirlwind.* She spent eighteen years in Stalin's camps. The Stalin-Hitler decades shaped my mind and I am still obsessed with the deliberate human degradation practiced by Russians and Germans on a vast scale. The passivity of the outside world during those terrible decades makes me scornful of the present fashionable agitation against all sorts of wrongs in non-communist countries. A world that did not raise its voice against the enormities of Stalin and Hitler is now crying out against injustice in Chile, Rhodesia and South Africa. Arnold Toynbee, who glowed when he shook Hitler's hand, called the displacement of Arabs by Israelis an atrocity greater than any committed by the Nazis.

In his *Autobiography*, John Nef says of the philosopher George Mead that "One thing that kept him from publishing as a philosopher was a strong belief that anything he wrote would no longer be true by the time it got into print." This suggests that contemporary philosophy is a fad that sooner or later goes out of date. The strange thing is that at present books based on facts rather than philosophical speculation are often overtaken by a similar fate. Facts have become as perishable as opinions. This holds true even of scientific facts. Only the human condition has remained timeless.

Authors

Harry Golden and Books

Ralph Waldo Emerson impressed me in my teens, and I will bet I have read *Miscellanies* twenty times since then. When a critic who reviewed my book *Only in America* said I was no Emerson, I was forced to write that the critic was no Edmund Wilson. I never set up as Emerson. Emerson is that American writer who means to me what Melville means to others and Mark Twain to still others. I venerated Emerson. I always wanted his picture up there on the classroom wall between Lincoln and Washington.

I loved school. I loved reading. I read everything I could about American and English history. I was as deeply interested in the War of the Roses as I was in the American Revolutionary War. Before I was fifteen, I had read Malory's *Morte d'Arthur* three times. I was taken with King Arthur and his knights. I have never stopped reading Malory and I think my affection for the *Morte d'Arthur* has had a genetic influence on my youngest son, Billy, a professor at the University of Florida, whose book *Confrontations* includes a systematic interpretation of the *Morte d'Arthur*.

Every Saturday morning I went to the Settlement House Library, where I read Jules Verne, Victor Hugo, Bulwer-Lytton, Dumas, and the Dick Hazzard series. There were books I could not give up even though I had read them several times. I carried *Enoch Arden* in my back pocket all one summer and learned how to read a book walking along the street as soldiers learn how to sleep when they march.

Authors

Richard Halliburton and Books

Princeton
11/30/20

I read all Saturday afternoon *A Vagabond Journey around the World*, for Mr. French is lecturing at L'ville soon and I'm to have dinner with him. Aren't you jealous, Dad? I must finish his book before then. I'll surely pump information from him.

I've read *Hamlet* for the fourth time (and shall many times again, as it is the most inexhaustible piece of literature), and written a 3000 word essay on "Hamlet before the First Act"—all since supper.

2/28/22

It's a very strong coincidence that today, the 28th of February, should be the very day I begin to read *Monte Cristo*, for in the story the two great events of the book Dante's imprisonment and liberation from the Chateau d'If, were both on February 28th. The book is all about Marseilles and Paris and I feel intimate toward it as if I were reading a book laid in Memphis or Princeton.

I enjoyed the *Innocents* more and more. Mark Twain had my idea exactly 50 years ago, but we cover different fields entirely and he is Mr. Twain and I'm only me, so he's in no danger! I like him best when he's serious. He is certainly a realist. But for his fine flight away from burlesque he might be successful in making people believe he was himself a boor, lacking sensitiveness and culture; always "in need of a spittoon," "of someone to take his muddy boots off the mantlepiece." Mark is right. His very carelessness and roughness are assets. I'll read more of him when I get home and study his later style.

Authors

Will Durant

Irene Walsh, aged twelve, had lent me, aged twelve, during calf-love idyl, her copy of *Pickwick Papers*; from that revelation dated my craze for books, which alarmed my parents and my teachers. St. Peter's College had a library temptingly rich in English literature; I prowled hungrily among those treasures, and then in the public libraries of Jersey City and Newark; in those avid seven days I must have read 2,000 books, some skippingly, some over and over again. I read almost every poem of Byron's, relished some wicked lines in *Don Juan*, and prayed to God to release him from hell; sure eighty years of burning were enough.

Studs Terkel

The Adventures of Huckleberry Finn taught me, in the words of Martin Luther King, "there is something beyond the written law; there is the law of human decency."

Authors

Whittaker Chambers and Darkness at Noon

Former Time Magazine Editor

"The characters in this book are fictitious. The historical circumstances which determined their actions are real. The life of the man N. S. Rubashov is a synthesis of the lives of a number of men who were victims of the so-called Moscow Trials. Several of them were personally known to the author. This book is dedicated to their memory.

–A. Koestler

Chambers wrote a few years ago to a friend: "If you re-read *Darkness at Noon* you will see how truly it is a book of poetry. I re-read it recently. I came to the part where after his breakdown, Rubashov is permitted a few minutes of air in the prison yard. Beside him trots the Central Asian peasant who was jailed because, at the pricking of the children, the peasant and his wife had barricaded themselves in their house and 'unmasked themselves as reactionaries.' Looking sideways at Rubashov in his sly peasant way, he says: 'I do not think they have left much of Your Honor and me.' Then, in the snows of the prison yard and under the machine-gun towers, he remembers how it was when the snow melted in the mountains of Asia, and flowed in torrent. Then they drove the sheep into the hills, rivers of them, 'so many that Your Honor could not count them all.' I cannot go on reading because I can no longer see the words. . . ."

Authors

Dale Carnegie: the Bible and Shakespeare

"But we have really left the best authors to the last. What are they? When Sir Henry Irving was asked to furnish a list of what he regarded as the hundred best books, he replied, 'Before a hundred books, commend me to the study of two – the Bible and Shakespeare.' Sir Henry was right. Drink from these two great fountain sources of English literature. Drink long and often. Toss your evening newspaper aside and say, 'Shakespeare, come here and talk to me tonight of Romeo and his Juliet, of Macbeth and his ambition.'

"If you do these things, what will be your reward? Gradually, unconsciously but inevitably, your diction will begin to take on added beauty and refinement. Gradually you will begin to reflect somewhat the glory and beauty and majesty of your companions. 'Tell me what you read,' observed Goethe, 'and I will tell you what you are.'

"This reading program that I have suggested will require little but will power little but a more careful husbanding of time. You can purchase pocket copies of Emerson's essays and Shakespeare's plays for fifty cents each."

Agatha Christie and Books

My mother, who had been passionately enthusiastic for education for girls, had now, characteristically, swung round to the opposite view. No child ought to be allowed to read until he was eight years old: better for the eyes and also for the brain.

Here, however, things did not go according to plan. When a story had been read to me and I liked it, I would ask for the book and study the pages which, at first meaningless, gradually began to make sense. When out with Nursie, I would ask her what the words written up over shops were. As a result, one day I found I was reading a book called *The Angel of Life* quite successfully to myself. I proceeded to do so out loud to Nursie.

"I'm afraid, ma'am," said Nursie apologetically to mother the next day, "Miss Agatha can read."

My mother was much distressed – but there it was. Not yet five, but the world of storybooks was open to me. From then on, for Christmas and birthdays I demanded books.

Illness and early death pervaded even children's books. A book called *Our White Violet* was a favorite of mine. *Little Women*, a cheerful tale on the whole, had to sacrifice rosy-faced Beth. The death of Little Nell in *The Old Curiosity Shop* leaves me cold and slightly nauseated, but in Dicken's time, of course, whole families wept over its pathos.

And there were, of course, the Old Testament stories, in which I had revelled from an early age.

Paterson, Doctor Stories

by William Carlos Williams
Recommended by: Robert Coles,
Professor, Dept. of Psychiatry, Harvard University

I wrote my major paper on Paterson. William Carlos Williams was, for me, (in his life and his work), both a refuge and a reprimand. For an activist, here was a man to emulate – a physician, a writer, a social historian; and to fear, if not find alarmingly "evil," because so unashamedly sensual.

Williams was no hero for a straitlaced, pious youth – "uptight," we'd now say. Or maybe he was just the hero needed. I found his prose and poetry brutally upsetting and confusing. I was scared enough, I now realize, to resort to psychological name-calling, well before I would possess the requisite technical vocabulary.

When I met the writing doc I learned that he earned, every day, his wide-eyed trenchant glimpses at all sorts of people, places, things. He was brusque, quick-tongued, impatient of cant. He was also extremely hard working, and obviously much beloved by hundreds of men, women, children: a street-wise city doc who had given his all to dozens and dozens of ordinary families, and who had managed, meanwhile, to learn from them so very much.

I suppose it was a flimsy reason to become a doctor – the wish to emulate a newly obtained hero – but I made it mine with a certain vengeance; well-developed Puritan instincts put to work once again, now in the service, however, of an explosive disregard of my earlier version of the very localism W. C. Williams so strenuously championed.

Literature and Life in America

Recommended by: T. Jack Colvin, CLU,
Vice President, Lamar Life Insurance

My favorite is *Literature and Life in America.* When I reached 17, I enlisted in the Navy. Dropping out of a vocational high school left a great void in my knowledge of American literature, and I still wanted to finish high school. I enrolled in an armed forces course in American literature. The assignments were quickly completed and mailed in, but the ship I was on suffered extensive damage from suicide planes and the exam was delayed.

The words of Franklin, Jefferson, Washington, Lincoln, Lee, Emerson, Thoreau, Longfellow, and a host of others came alive and encouraged me. When I was transferred from the damaged ship to a remote area of the Aleutians, there was time to muse over Lowell, Whittier, Poe, Whitman, Lanier and others. Almost as if by chance, I passed the educational officer's office. I stood at the door wondering what use it was; would this be just another disappointment? Finally, with great reluctance, I turned the door knob and asked about taking the long delayed literature course exam.

The officer, a former high school teacher, quickly recognized my need was for more than just an exam. He picked up my sagging spirits and gave me the confidence to complete high school and to take the college entrance exams. His encouragement led me to a college diploma, something I thought was beyond my fondest dreams.

Yes, books do change lives, and *Literature and Life in America*, its pages turning brown with age, holds an important spot in my life and in my library.

As a Man Thinketh

by James Allen
Recommended by: Robert Conklin, CPAE, President, Conklin Company

I had spent most of my life in a classroom with only a few short years in the sales world when a wondrous little book came into my hands.

At the time, I was a newly appointed sales manager anxiously searching for the hidden formulas that would turn my sales dwarfs into giants.

The way, I discovered, to succeed in selling or in any of life's endeavors, is so obvious it is almost lost in complete oblivion.

James Allen expressed it simply and beautifully in *As a Man Thinketh*. Life is an extension of thought. One will not only experience what one thinks, but it will form "the outer garment of circumstances."

Allen likens the mind to a garden. What is planted will infallibly be grown into the condition of life. The soil doesn't care whether the seeds are weeds or flowers. It will render whatever is planted.

So it is with the mind. Positive thoughts will furnish positive results, negative thoughts will furnish negative results.

How can any fault be found with words as wondrously meaningful as these: "Man reveals, within himself, the laws of thought, and understands, with ever-increasing accuracy, how the thought-forces and mind-elements operate in the shaping of his character, circumstances, and destiny."

How to Stop Worrying and Start Living

by Dale Carnegie
Recommended by: Jerry J. Cornwell, CPA
Singer, Lewak, Greenbaum & Goldstein

How to Stop Worrying and Start Living had a large impact upon my life from the moment I first read it in 1970. Since that time I have read the book many times and applied it in my everyday life. Although it was written in 1944, this book is still relevant today. Its contents have helped me avoid burn-out, which frequently happens to people in my stressful occupation. The book contains almost an endless number of notable quotes. I will highlight only a few which have had an impact on me.

"Shut the iron doors on the past and the future. Live in day tight compartments."

"Businessmen who do not know how to fight worry, die young."

"Confusion is the chief cause of worry."

"We have to keep our emotions out of our thinking."

"What are the chances, according to the law of averages, that this event I am worrying about will ever occur?"

"Let's never waste a minute thinking about people we don't like."

"Think and act cheerfully and you will feel cheerful."

"Cooperate with the inevitable."

"The tendency to seldom think of what we have but always of what we lack is the greatest tragedy on earth. Count your blessings – not your troubles!"

"When fate hands us a lemon, let's try to make a lemonade."

"No matter what happens, always be yourself!"

Unconditional Love

by John Powell
Recommended by: Tim Connor,
President, TR Training Associates

True unconditional love is you love someone because their heart is beating, and even after it stops, regardless of behavior. John Powell in this wonderful book is pointing the way, please read it today.

True love is unconditional. There is no third possibility: love is either conditional or unconditional. Either I attach conditions to my love for you or I do not. To the extent that I do attach such conditions, I do not really love you. I am only offering an exchange, not a gift. And true love is and must always be a free gift.

The gift of my love means this: I want to share with you whatever I have that is good. You did not win a contest or prove yourself worthy of this gift. It is not a question of deserving my love. I have no delusions that either of us is the best person in the world. I do not even suppose that, of all the available persons, we are the most compatible. I am sure that somewhere there is someone who would be "better" for you or for me. All that is really not to the point. The point is that I have chosen to give you my gift of love and you have chosen to love me. This is the only soil in which love can possibly grow. "We're gonna make it together!"

Hope for the Flowers

by Trina Paulus
Recommended by: Wayne Cotton, CLU, Cotton Planning Service Ltd., Canada

I wept when I read *Hope for the Flowers*. This simple allegory about a caterpillar is really a significant story about life. Trina Paulus' writing helped me learn to quit struggling for achievement by trying to be on the same path as everyone else.

The impact of this simple, beautiful book has been incredible for me. I've learned to do my own thing . . . to be what I alone can be . . . and not to worry about being a part of the crowd.

If you like butterflies and want to "fly high," be sure to read this book. It will help you understand there is so much more to life than being a part of the dictates of the system of success we often tout as "the way."

Caterpillars have the most fascinating discussions about their struggles for survival:

"Do you know what's happening?"

"I just arrived myself," said the other. "Nobody has time to explain; they're so busy trying to get wherever they're going – up there."

"But what's at the top?" continued Stripe.

"No one knows that either but it must be awfully good because everybody's rushing there. Goodbye; I've no more time!"

The Go-Getter

by Peter B. Kyne
Recommended by: Reginald Couch,
President, Avante International, Inc.

Twenty years ago I was introduced to a book called *The Go-Getter*, by Peter B. Kyne. I have probably reread the book over a dozen times. More importantly, I have quoted from it hundreds of times.

In spite of its brevity and the simplicity of its story, this book inspired me to be a go-getter.

In turn, I have given a copy of this book to each of my associates and encouraged them to be go-getters as well. The author writes:

"This little book is dedicated to the memory of my dead chief, Brigadier-General Leroy S. Lyon, sometime commander of the 65th Field Artillery Brigade, 40th Division, United States Army.

"He practiced and preached a religion of loyalty to the country and the appointed task, whatever it might be."

Born Rich

by Bob Proctor
Recommended by: Jack Craig,
President, Marketing Associates, Canada

Born Rich outlines a plan – a very simple plan – that will take you from where you are to where you want to be. Each successive chapter is designed to lift the reader to a greater awareness of one's true self and true abilities.

All of us have been "born rich" in the sense of having a magnificent, God-given potential which we owe it to ourselves to nurture. The rewards we will enjoy in life will not come because of our potential but, rather, because of our performance.

"Those who know the truth learn to love it, those who love the truth learn to live it."

"Consciousness is and always has been developed through thinking."

"If you can show me a person who achieves great things, I can show you a person who has great faith in himself and in his ability to achieve what he images."

"There never is and there never has been any lack of supply."

"What you expect – that is what you attract – that is what you ultimately receive."

"Failing does not make us a failure."

"The law of attraction is the underlying principle which governs the level of your personal prosperity."

"Great achievers always expect to do great things."

On Wings of Eagles

by Ken Follett
Recommended by: John Jay Daly,
President, John Jay Daly Association

Beautifully organized, perhaps reflecting the author's association with Ross Perot, this book opens with a listing of "The Cast of Characters" and concludes with both an Epilogue and an Appendix, plus a well-deserved Acknowledgement that even includes thanks to those who transcribed countless hours of taped interviews.

In between, Ken Follett has managed to capture dialogue and a sense of drama that would do credit to us all. Suffice it to say readers get the feeling of being where the tensions mounted in Iran till they exploded, resulting in the capture of a key Electronic Data Systems team in Teheran. Feeling personally betrayed by the government's change of tactics, Perot went to the highest levels in Washington to exert pressure for his employees' release. Not getting satisfaction, and feeling increasing frustration, he took the rescue mission into his own hands.

Sparing no expense, he hired topnotch soldiers-of-fortune, paid them well and gave them totally free rein to accomplish the sensitive mission. All of this occurred months before the more famous capture of U.S. Embassy personnel, but the ill-fated rescuers who worked on that unsuccessful escape should have taken a leaf or two from Perot's book. Follett paints word pictures and recounts conversations that bring the entire episode alive, reflecting time and again Perot's deep concern for the safety of the prisoners and the ultimate welfare of those who are trying to rescue them.

Noodles Du Jour

by Wally Armbruster
Recommended by: Jerome R. Davis,
President, Davis Communications, Inc.

Noodles Du Jour by Wally Armbruster is a picker-upper with a catchy idea and an illustration on every page. It's for every day. You can start on any page. It's spiral bound and can hang on a wall or sit on a desk or table. It reminds me that each day is full of potential. The following are some quotes:

"Which is prettier – a butterfly or a frog? Oh yeah, not if you're a frog!"

"When you look at the pretty flowers – do you take time to look at a flower?"

"Let's begin TODAY by thinking of the people who bring in food – the farmers who grow it AND the truck drivers who haul it AND the people in the stores who sell it."

"It's not all bad if you get mad at God. It at least shows you really believe in Him."

"Do you think God has a sense of humor? HA! HA! If he doesn't, we're in bad shape!"

"The people who have the most demanding bosses are those who are self-employed."

These are examples of noodles of the day. What is a noodle? Our author, Wally Armbruster, tells us. "What is a noodle? It's just like a doodle, only just the opposite. Doodles are things you do without thinking anything – noodles are things you think without doing anything."

The Greatest Salesman in the World

by Og Mandino
Recommended by: Dave Dean, Author, Professional Speaker

Og Mandino's *The Greatest Salesman in the World* had a transforming effect on my life.

For the first time in my life, I could honestly understand how some people that lack faith in God could give up on themselves and end life altogether.

It was at that point that Og's book, *The Greatest Salesman in the World*, had a profound influence on me. I was selling books door-to-door again with The Southwestern Company in Nashville, Tennessee, for the summer. I found my direction and inspiration in two sources: The Bible and Og Mandino's book. I prayed daily and lived with the principles from *The Greatest Salesman in the World*. It never failed to give me inspiration, confidence, hope, peace of mind, and a belief that with the good Lord's help and a lot of hard work a comeback was possible. By following the philosophy so simply and skillfully presented, I developed persistence, a sense of humor, a love for people and a real sense of purpose and urgency.

During my next thirteen years with Southwestern, over 50,000 of our salespeople read this classic. We felt so strongly about the positive influence *The Greatest Salesman in the World* was having that it became an automatic part of the material our salespeople received in starting their sales careers.

Musicians and Books

Andre Kostelanetz and Mark Twain

Some years ago I came across an observation of Mark Twain's: "The secret source of Humor itself is not joy but sorrow. There is no humor in heaven." It was one of those declarations I've encountered from time to time that seem to carry the ring of absolute truth because they correspond instantly to my own experience. During the war I marveled at the number of funny stories in continuous mass circulation. Instinctively people turned to humor for comfort, for relief from the daily assault on their sensibilities. You had only to look, and humor was there. The most seriously motivated endeavor would almost inevitably be punctuated with a humorous exclamation point–and another anecdote lovingly added to the trove.

Arthur Rubinstein and Books

My parents became increasingly worried about my brooding and my aversion to school. I even neglected the piano, and Mr. Prechner complained about my inattentiveness and laziness. The only thing I liked was reading, and I would consume anything I could put my hands on; the novels of Sienkiewicz, Jules Verne, fairy tales, history, and biographies of famous men were my favorites. But not poetry; to me poetry was sham music, a sort of "music's poor relation."

I must confess that ever since my old Altmann days I have read every philosopher within reach. I admired Kant's logic. I enjoyed Nietzsche's lofty, exalted mind, and Bergson's serenity and clear-cut sentences; Schopenhauer's pessimistic utterances about women disquieted me, but none of them ever seriously influenced me in any way. I was determined to look at life with my own eyes and to have the courage to face it.

Running & Being– The Total Experience

by Dr. George Sheehan
Recommended by: Keith DeGreen, Author, Certified Speaking Professional

You don't have to love running to love this wonderful book. Here are a few of the gems of thought Dr. Sheehan gave me:

"The weakest among us can become some kind of athlete, but only the strongest can survive as spectators."

"The intellect must surely harden as fast as the arteries. Creativity depends on action. Trust no thought arrived at sitting down."

I hadn't touched this book for five years. But while flipping through its time-worn pages recently, I was again recaptured. Sheehan has far less to say about avoiding shin splints than he has to say about our inherent greatness.

My many underlinings in the book are a happy reminder of how the author touched me; and this notation to myself on the title page is evidence of how he challenged me:

"Is it true the older a man gets the more intensely he regrets his past?"

I still don't know.

I think I'll go jogging.

A Case for Believing

by James Dillet Freeman
Recommended by: Joy de Montaigne,
Professional Speaker

To Be or Not To Be. . . .

These words are simple in their individual form yet complex when forming a question. As a question they create the need for inquiry into the minds and hearts of those who see them, hear them, speak them and think them.

One may inquire of themselves whether TO BE a Believer or NOT TO BE a Believer. The decision depends upon what or whom is involved in the decision making process.

This is *A Case for Believing*. Believing in oneself, one's mate, family, friends, business associates, prospects, clientele and every stranger just waiting to become a friend. Believing in Creation and its Creator, God, Who is in all as all.

Freeman's *A Case for Believing* begins with the "Beachhead In The Unknown" and takes us on a wonderful journey through Life and the special qualities that give it meaning. We are given a multitude of reasons to believe as we are taken through "The Age Of Machinery," and "The Unmachine," into a world where "One and Two Make Four."

We are challenged by "The Law of Survival" where there is "Deep Meaning and Great Worth."

We are challenged by an Act of Faith in the final chapter as we read and learn of "The Music Maker."

I have made the journey and now have my Case For Believing and I believe that all who read this inspiring, entertaining yet probing book will be stimulated to make their own Case For Believing.

The Last Lion

by William Manchester
Recommended by: Donald Dick, Insurance Executive, Canada

I chose this biography as one with a profound effect on me, because after reading this account of the great man's life, I felt Winston Churchill to be the most outstanding human being of the century, or at least the half-century.

From the very beginning of his life, in spite of a terrible parent-child relationship, he showed the evidence of a strong personal faith and belief in God. He was almost totally rejected by disinterested, preoccupied parents. He wrote innumerable letters from boarding school pleading with his mother to visit him at Christmas (this being when he was 11–14). The letters either went unanswered or the replies failed to refer to any plans of the family being together at Christmas. Young Winston spent Christmases alone at a school where all the other students were away with their families for the holidays.

It is astounding that with his incredibly unfortunate childhood – coupled with a continued series of failures at school and, later, political failure upon failure – that this man would show such greatness in his country's finest hour.

Time may dim the memory of those blackest days of mankind known as World War II, but I think we may have some small insight of greatness of "The Man" when we read of his speech to a graduating class at Harrow. At 80 years of age, he stood, looked over his glasses, continued without a sound to look at the young graduates gathered and then simply said, "Never, Never, Never Give Up!" – then sat down.

Insurance Executives

My Utmost for His Highest

by Oswald Chambers
Recommended by: Robert Schuefler
Dallas, Texas

The Healing Heart

by Norman Cousins
Recommended by: Bernard Roseman,
Providence, Rhode Island

Churchill, the Last Lion

by William Manchester
Recommended by: Stanley Stone,
Florida Assoc. of Life Underwriters

The book I would certainly recommend is: *Churchill, the Last Lion*, by William Manchester. Manchester is undoubtedly one of the nation's most prolific authors, and his sincere tribute by him to the former Prime Minister is an absolute jewel of penetrating research and in-depth analysis, done in superlative style. As you read the book, you can almost imagine the people from that era as they lived, toiled and cut a huge swath through world history.

The One Minute Manager

by Kenneth Blanchard & Spencer Johnson
Recommended by: William Wallace, CLU,
Washington, D.C.

Marshall: Hero of Our Times

by Leonard Mosely
Recommended by: J. Smith Ferebee
Richmond, Virginia

Frederick Douglass and a Book

When I was thirteen years old, I had earned a little money in blacking boots for some gentlemen, with which I purchased of Mr. Knight, on Thames Street, what was then a very popular school book, viz., *The Columbian Orator*, for which I paid fifty cents. I was led to buy this book by hearing some little boys say they were going to learn some pieces out of it for the exhibition.

I met here one of Sheridan's mighty speeches, on the subject of Catholic Emancipation, Lord Chatham's speech on the American War, and speeches by the great William Pitt, and by Fox. These were all choice documents to me, and I read them over and over again, with an interest ever increasing, because it was ever gaining in intelligence; for the more I read them the better I understood them. The reading of these speeches added much to my limited stock of language, and enabled me to give tongue to many interesting thoughts which had often flashed through my mind and died away for want of words in which to give them utterance.

With a book in my hand so redolent of the principles of liberty, with a perception of my own human nature and the facts of my past and present experience, I was equal to a contest with the religious advocates of slavery, whether white or black, for blindness in this matter was not confined to the white people.

Executives

Management Development

by Robert House
Recommended by: John H. Duncan,
Senior Vice-President, Eastman, Inc.

I am delighted to recommend a book which I feel has had an important influence on my personal management development. Robert House authored a book entitled *Management Development*. This is a 110-page review on this subject and was written quite a few years ago while he was at the University of Michigan.

Being a fast reader, I assumed that I could finish such a book in perhaps an hour or so. I spent an entire weekend digesting the most meaningful information I have seen on the principles of scientific management.

The central theme expresses a problem . . . "Growing companies never have the right amount of good managers at the right time." The book then describes solutions which emphasize planned internal development.

The One Minute Manager

by Kenneth Blanchard & Spencer Johnson
Recommended by: Richard G. Gretz,
Vice-President, Spring-Green Lawn Care Corp.

The One Minute Manager by Blanchard and Johnson is a book I believe all people should read. It breaks into the most simple terms not only how to be a more effective manager in business but also how to be a more caring, appreciative, and effective leader in life. They present goal setting, reprimanding, and praising as cornerstones to better living and loving.

What a super little book!

Executives

The Greatest Salesman in the World

by Og Mandino
Recommended by: Larry Milner,
Vice-President, Southwestern Public Service

Life Is Tremendous

by Charles T. Jones
Recommended by: Spencer Hays,
Exec. Chairman, The Southwestern Company

The One Minute Manager

by Kenneth Blanchard and Spencer Johnson
Recommended by: Robert J. Steele,
Vice-President, AMP Incorporated

Power Broker: Robert Moses & the Fall of New York

by Robert A. Caro
Recommended by: Don Derr,
Sales Executive, Vernon Company

How to Get People to Do Things

by Robert Conklin
Recommended by: Jake Dyck,
Insurance Executive, Canada

Robert Conklin's book, *How to Get People to Do Things*, is highly recommended for people of all walks of life who want to grow. The author tells us the causes of frustration, irritation, and aggravation and how to deal with them. He tells us, "to get people to do things – you must scratch them where they itch."

Mr. Conklin tells us that "Behavior is shaped by emotions." "They make the mistake of assuming that others do things from logic, reason, and intelligence. But that's not true. Human beings act emotionally. And emotions defy analysis, judgment, and reason. We are intellectual, yes, but not intellectually directed. People are moved and motivated by emotions. Living is a constant process of trying to satisfy emotional needs and wants. Intellect and logic do not motivate. Emotion does. How do you talk to emotions? Gently. Patiently. Persuasively. With empathy. That means putting yourself in the other person's situation, trying to feel as you imagine that person feels."

"When you want to convert someone to your view, you go over to where he is standing, take him by the hand (mentally speaking), and guide him. You start where he is, and work from that position. That's the only way to get him to budge. People are like the calf. You can poke them, prod them, push them, and they don't move. But give them a good reason – one of their reasons – a way in which they benefit, and they will follow gently along. To persuade people to do anything, you must talk in terms of need – emotional benefit to them!"

Grow Rich with Peace of Mind

by Napoleon Hill
Recommended by: Joyce Eddy,
President, Habersham Plantation Furniture

One of the many great illustrations in this book is: don't grab for wealth, earn it and share it:

"The R. G. LeTourneau Company is a large employer. Some years ago I received a phone call from a former student who had become one of its executives. 'Please come to see us immediately. We have a difficulty which only you can handle.'

"When I arrived at the LeTourneau plant I learned that communistic influences had entered in the guise of a labor union. The company wanted help in immunizing its employees against this 'ism,' knowing that if the crisis could be surmounted the men would realize which way of life was best for them.

"They asked me my fee. 'Perhaps there will be no fee. Give me freedom to act, and if I cannot overcome your trouble there will be no charge. If I succeed in eliminating the communistic influences. I'll tell you later what my fee will be.'

"The deal was closed on that basis. I set up a cot in the plant and stayed on duty day and night.

"I succeeded. When I named my compensation, I received it immediately. Eight months later the company increased my fee. Thus it goes when men realize that wealth is not something you grab from another; it is something you build for yourself out of service to others, sparked and enhanced by your own positive, joyful inward drive. This is true wealth and part of peace of mind. I do not know how many of those LeTourneau men became rich, but I know they had reason to bear in mind the true picture of wealth and share it with others."

Thomas Edison and Books

"My refuge was the Detroit Public Library. I started with the first book on the bottom shelf and went through the lot, one by one. I didn't read a few books. I read the library. Then I got the collection called *The Penny Library Encyclopedia* and read that through . . . I read Burton's *Anatomy of Melancholy*–pretty heavy reading for a youngster. It might have been if I hadn't been taught by my deafness that I could enjoy any good literature. . . . Following the *Anatomy* came Newton's *Principles*. . . ."

He had formerly read at random books of history, literature, and elementary science, under his mother's tutelage, in an indiscriminate fashion. Now, going it alone, he carried on a sort of frontal attack on books of every sort. Robert Burton, the old seventeenth-century ecclesiastic, on one day, Isaac Newton the next! The title and theme of Burton's whimsical work must have appealed to Tom Edison's mood at this stage; Burton, too, felt himself isolated, sang of his loneliness and poverty, and also of his dreams, of his will to happiness, though in the simplest and humblest circumstances.

Edison vastly enjoyed reading Victor Hugo's romantic epic *Les Miserables*, just then translated into English and being very widely read in the United States. The story of the lost children, such as Gavroche, and the figure of the noblehearted ex-convict, Jean Valjean (also an "outsider"), appealed to him strongly. In his youth he spoke of Hugo with such enthusiasm that his companions sometimes called him "Victor Hugo" Edison.

The Critical Path to Sales Success

by Frank E. Sullivan
Recommended by: Grant Fairly, C.L.U., Insurance Exec., Past President—Canadian Life Underwriters Association

"T. S. Eliot said the end precedes the beginning. You can't have a race without first having a finish line. That's why it is logical to end with the first step on the critical path. Establishing goals is the alpha and the omega. In establishing goals, we are accepting our responsibility to achieve success in our careers.

"Our responsibilities do not end there. Business success is only the beginning. Successful salesmen have a deep obligation to the future of selling as a livelihood. As leaders, they must go where the action is and lead. They must accept the obligation of attracting capable young men to this business. They should also devote some time to encouraging young men who are now struggling to become successful. These young men are the leaders of tomorrow. Their capability as leaders depends on how early in their careers they are helped. Frequently, just a brief period of concerned listening to a young man's problems enables an experienced salesman to give him a suggestion that can accelerate his progress. Every ambitious young salesman deserves the opportunity to be exposed to the methods of successful men."

Give Them Hell, Harry

by Merle Mitchell
Recommended by: Tom Faranda,
President, Faranda & Associates

In reading this book, what constantly impressed me about Harry Truman was his overwhelming integrity and decision-making ability. The man was an exceptional leader.

Managers today live in a far-reaching and complex world. If ever skills of decision-making and leadership were needed, it is today and tomorrow. These skills, combined with integrity, provide the type of managers we need in industry, in politics, and in society in general.

"But to me his greatest quality as President, as a leader, was his ability to decide. General Marshall, who also had that quality, has said that the ability to make a decision is a great gift, perhaps the greatest gift a man can have. And Mr. Truman had that gift in abundance. When I would come to him with a problem, the only question he ever asked was, 'How long have I got?' And he never asked later what would have happened if he had decided differently. I doubt that that ever concerned him. He was not a man who was tortured by second thoughts. Those were luxuries, like self-pity, in which a man in power could not indulge himself."

Magnificent Obsession

by Lloyd C. Douglas
Recommended by: Art Fettig,
President, Growth Unlimited, Inc.

There are over a thousand books in my personal library and I vowed that I would not walk out of that room until I had selected just one book that had greatly influenced my life. It took several trips into that room before I could settle on just one book and it turned out to be an old novel. I reread the book and felt it was dated. The story line just didn't seem right now. But I remember back when I read it that I was hurting inside. A failure in my own mind. Going nowhere with my life. And the message was simple. That living should be the challenge of giving and not of getting.

Find people in need and fill that need with the contract that they will not try to repay you, that they will not tell anyone that you helped them, that you too promise not to tell anyone about this kind deed and that, when the situation changes and the other party finds someone in need, that they might help they will practice this same kind of loving.

I tried it and it changed my life. And now I write books and give speeches and the more I give to others the more the Lord blesses me.

As a piece of writing, *Magnificent Obsession* is a model for me. Take a great truth and cloak it in the manner of fiction. Teach this truth to your characters after a long struggle and perhaps you will teach your readers in a way that will stick in their minds for a lifetime.

With me, the message of *Magnificent Obsession* stuck.

Compensation

by Ralph Waldo Emerson
Recommended by: Ben B. Franklin,
Vice-President, Associated Dinner Clubs

In his Essay on *Compensation*, Emerson told me that, "the compensations of calamity are made apparent to the understanding also, after long interval of time. A fever, a mutilation, a cruel disappointment, a loss of wealth, a loss of friends, seems at the moment unpaid loss, and unpayable. But the sure years reveal the deep remedial force that underlies all facts . . . it commonly operates revolutions in our way of life, terminates an epoch of infancy or of youth which was waiting to be closed, breaks up a wonted occupation, or a household, or style of living, and allows the formation of new ones more friendly to the growth of character."

I was born and reared in Topeka, Kansas, spending a normal childhood there. In 1962 I went off to the University of Colorado in Boulder. Less than a year later, on April 14, 1963, I was mountain-climbing with two friends when my rope broke. I fell more than 100 feet down the face of the cliff, breaking my back in four places and my pelvis in two. The broken vertebrae hit my spinal cord, and I was left paralyzed from the waist down for the rest of my life. I was 18 years old at the time.

For the next two years I poured out my pounding prayers to God – asking Him why.

"Why, God? Why me? Why can't I move my legs? Why this injustice, this massive pain, this bitter humiliation to me?" It wasn't until I met Ralph Waldo Emerson that I received the answers to these prayers.

How to Put More Time in Your Life

by Dru Scott, Ph.D.
Recommended by: Patricia Fripp, CPAE, Certified Speaking Professional President of National Speakers Association

The best time management book I have read is Dru Scott's *How to Put More Time in Your Life*. Not only does she teach us specific techniques but she goes further than most time management teachers. Dr. Scott looks at the psychological reasons why we waste time. The five compulsive time personalities she says are: Hurry-up: People playing a hurry-up role always rush whether it's necessary or not. The next type is Be Perfect. People who play a be perfect role waste valuable time on trivial or marginal matters because they feel they must perform every task perfectly. The third one is Please Me. Do you often say yes when you want to say no? If so, you're probably playing a please me role. Please me types often have the best intentions in the world. They don't want to hurt someone's feelings. The fourth role is Try Hards. People who play try hard roles, do a lot of sighing. They thrive on suffering and talk constantly about how hard they work. Be Strongs are the fifth. Traditional time management techniques often work for the be strong type. These methods emphasize discipline and unemotional evaluation.

I found this book and this information fascinating and useful and I would encourage anyone who wants to get what they want to read Dru Scott's *How to Put More Time in Your Life*.

Mahatma Gandhi and a Book

As a boy Gandhi was studying so hard that he had little time for reading books outside the school curriculum, but a book called *Shravana Pitribakhti* (Shravana's Love for His Father) found in his father's library, made a deep impression. It was a drama describing how the youthful hero Shravana went on a pilgrimage, carrying his blind parents in baskets which hung from a yoke across his shoulders. Finally, after many adventures, the hero went to fetch water from a river, and he was killed by the king, who mistook the sound of water filling the pitcher for the sound of an elephant drinking. The bereaved and helpless parents lamented over his dead body. Some time later Mohandas saw some itinerant showmen performing the play with slides in a steropticon to accompaniment of musical instruments. He was especially enthralled by the song of the lamenting parents, which he learned to sing while playing on a concertina. In the play he found confirmation for his absolute devotion to his parents. He would live for them and die for them and nothing would be permitted to come between him and them.

–Robert Payne

A Man Called Peter

by Catherine Marshall
Recommended by: Bobbie Gee,
President, Bobbie Gee Enterprises

What a joy and pleasure it has been for me to once again read *A Man Called Peter*. I read it the first time twenty-five years ago, and it had a tremendous impact on my life. I was greatly impressed with the quality and success of this man's life—his zest for living and his zest for the moral principles he believed in. He taught me that God wants us to be good . . . not goody-goody.

It is hard to say what it was that had such an effect on me. Peter Marshall was considered one of the great orators of his time. He could speak so well that he held audiences spellbound. Publications constantly asked for copies of his sermons and speeches, and yet one friend commented, "One of Peter's great qualities, in the midst of all the acclaim and adulation which he received, was that he never lost his deep sense of humility. He was a man of faith and courage, who lived what he believed no matter what others thought."

In 1947, Peter Marshall became chaplain of the United States Senate. He lived by strict moral principles, but he had fun doing it. No matter how busy he was, other people's needs always had priority on his time. As a young mother, this taught me that no matter how busy I was, or thought I was, the needs of my family were more important. This has given me many valuable moments with my daughters.

Success!

by Michael Korda
Recommended by: Major David Glaspell, U.S. National Guard

"Invariably, we know far more than we think we know. We have simply decided that a large part of our knowledge is either useless or counterproductive. Successful people tap these reserves of knowledge, and consider nothing useless. And what they know well, they concentrate on and put to use.

"Second only to loyalty is the ability to take on responsibility. Success on any major scale requires you to accept responsibility. You have to assume all the problems, difficulties and doubts of other people, and to reflect back your capacity for decision-making and action, and for enduring without visible signs of worry or panic.

"The best way to succeed is to take on responsibility quietly. The determination to take on responsibility implies a certain humility at the beginning. You may have to take on unwelcome chores, sometimes even degrading ones. It doesn't matter. Seek for things that you can get done even if it's only firing people nobody else wants to face.

"The freedom to fail is vital if you're going to succeed. Most successful men fail time and time again, and it is a measure of their strength that failure merely propels them into some new attempt at success."

Psycho-Cybernetics

by Dr. Maxwell Maltz
Recommended by: C. Robert Hammer, CLU
Insurance Executive

I have always enjoyed reading, particularly books on the '30s through World War II, biographies, and sports. However, if I had to choose one book to always be with me, I would have to choose *Psycho-Cybernetics*. There are many parts of the book I constantly refer to, such as "30 Minute Exercise," "Rules to Follow," "Success-type Personality," and "Forgive Yourself."

"As I use it, 'success' has nothing to do with prestige symbols, but with creative accomplishment. Rightly speaking no man should attempt to be 'a success,' but every man can and should attempt to be 'successful.' Trying to be 'a success' in terms of acquiring prestige symbols and wearing certain badges leads to neuroticism, and frustration and unhappiness. Striving to be 'successful' brings not only material success, but satisfaction, fulfillment and happiness.

"Noah Webster defined success as 'the satisfactory accomplishment of a goal sought for.' Creative striving for a goal that is important to you as a result of your own deep-felt needs, aspirations and talents (and not the symbols which the 'Joneses' expect you to display) brings happiness as well as success because you will be functioning as you were meant to function. Man is by nature a goal-striving being. And because man is 'built that way' he is not happy unless he is functioning as he was made to function – as a goal-striver. Thus true success and true happiness not only go together but each enhances the other."

Resurrection

by Neville
Recommended by: Mark V. Hansen,
Certified Speaking Professional, Author

A book that has had a profound and lasting effect on my personal growth and spiritual development is *Resurrection*, by Neville, published by DeVorss, Santa Monica, CA. Neville is the greatest writer-teacher of the principle of visualization that I have ever read. He shares his personal experiences and results in a thought-provoking way such that one can immediately apply this great conceptual, result-getting principle.

Research scientists say that 87% of the mind is visually oriented to the imagery that we put into it. Neville clearly explains how to effectively tap into our own infinitely resourceful human-bio-computer to be what we want to be, do what we want to do, and have what we want to have.

I totally recommend this great book to every person who wants to be all that they can be.

The Road Less Traveled

by Dr. Scott Peck
Recommended by: Mark O. Haroldson, Author, Professional Speaker

This is a book about Love, Relationships, Problems, Dependency-manipulation, etc. An excellent book, it helped me through a difficult part of my life.

"So original sin does exist; it is our laziness. It is very real. It exists in each and every one of us—infants, children, adolescents, mature adults, the elderly; the wise or the stupid; the lame or the whole. Some of us may be less lazy than others, but we are all lazy to some extent. No matter how energetic, ambitious or even wise we may be, if we truly look into ourselves we will find laziness lurking at some level. It is the force of entropy within us, pushing us down and holding us all back from our spiritual evolution.

"No words can be said, no teaching can be taught that will relieve spiritual travelers from the necessity of picking their own ways, working out with effort and anxiety their own paths through the unique circumstances of their own lives toward the identification of their individual selves with God."

Man of Steel & Velvet

by Aubrey P. Andelin
Recommended by: Fred Harteis,
President, Harteis International, Inc.

This book is one of the most needed books in America today. Our society needs leadership and accountability from its men. We see far too much family strife from a lack of direction by the men. Women's liberation is not a result of domineering American women but a result of a lack of leadership and responsibility of the men to provide, protect, and love their families.

Until a man has his personal life right, nothing in his life will be right. Andelin has a refreshing, forthright way of explaining what it takes to be a man among his family and a man among men. He discusses practical solutions in marriage, and understanding women, and gives common sense ideas which will win admiration and cooperation in the home:

"There is a masculine pride in connection with a man's responsibility to provide the living which is inborn in a real man. He accepts his obligation with a willingness of spirit, regardless of the difficulties encountered. He is not a leaner; he is not looking for someone else to carry his burdens or to do what he is charged with doing. This natural instinct is not a vain weakness in men, but is implanted in them by God for a divine purpose – to assure that families will be adequately provided for."

The Weight of Glory and Other Addresses

by C. S. Lewis
Recommended by: Wesley E. Harty, Educator, Bible Teacher

There are few of us in Christian service who wouldn't list C. S. Lewis's writings as among those books which have had a profound effect on our ministries. The one that I keep reading and quoting from is not one of Lewis's "biggies." It's a little sixty-six paper entitled *The Weight of Glory and Other Addresses*, a title almost as long as the book itself.

Within those few pages are five essays containing absolute gems of insight and wisdom that keep me coming back again and again to the slender little volume. For instance, when Lewis discusses the question of our being glorified by God he startles you with thoughts like these:

"The promise of glory is the promise, almost incredible, and only possible by the work of Christ, that some of us, that any of us who really chooses, shall actually survive (God's) examination, shall find approval, shall please God. To please God . . . to be a real ingredient in the divine happiness . . . to be loved by God, not merely pitied, but delighted in as an artist delights in his work or a father in a son–it seems impossible, a weight or burden of glory which our thoughts can hardly sustain. But so it is."

In his address entitled "Membership" he considers the relationship between personal identity and the Church. (Do you know anyone else who links those two ideas together?)

The Magic of Believing

by Claude Bristol
Recommended by: Roy Hatten, CPAE
Professional Speaker

In 1949, a very wise boss of mine handed me a book by Claude Bristol called *The Magic of Believing*. I consumed the book and realized that if I were to be successful in life, I would have to revise my thinking. I learned that attitudes are free, but my choice could be expensive.

Negative and positive attitudes both work. My life was a matter of which choice I made. Negative thinkers are like a defensive football team. They don't even have the ball, all they try to do is prevent. Positive thinkers are like the offensive team, they have the ball and are deciding what to do with it in order to score.

I was led to many other books that reinforced what I learned from Claude Bristol. His book was the major turning point in my life. My Bible is my favorite book, which I call my "Manufacturers Handbook."

From it, I learned that the words we utter out of our mouths are programmed into our computer and, as Jesus said in Mark 11:23, "He shall have whatsoever he saith." You can identify personally with that if you have ever said, "I can remember faces, but I can't remember names." What has been the result of what you said? You got it. I have been speaking and teaching on this subject for over thirty years and I have seen it change lives. Thank God for books.

The Go-Getter

by Peter B. Kyne

Recommended by: Ira M. Hayes, CPAE, Certified Speaking Professional, Past President of National Speakers Association

I was first introduced to this book several years ago when the company I was with at that time, NCR Corporation, used it as part of a sales contest.

I had never heard of it. I read it. I've never forgotten it.

It's a little book with a huge message. It's about a man who faces unimaginable obstacles but gets the job done.

It's about dedication, discipline, loyalty and commitment, reflected in these words of the Go-Getter in the book, Mr. Bill Peck:

"You told me what to do but you did not insult my intelligence by telling me how to do it. When my late brigadier sent me after the German sniper he didn't take into consideration that the sniper might get me. He told me to get the sniper. It was my business to see to it that I accomplished my mission and carried my objective, which, of course, I could not have done if I had permitted the German to get me."

No, the book is not about fighting wars. It's about the exciting, unbelievable lengths a man goes to, to find a "blue vase."

"It's a cloisonne vase, Bill – sort of old dutch blue, or delft, with some oriental funny-business on it. I couldn't describe it exactly, but it has some birds and flowers on it. It's about a foot tall and four inches in diameter and sets on a teak-wood base."

"Very well, sir, you shall have it."

Everyone should read *The Go-Getter*.

Success through a Positive Mental Attitude

by Napoleon Hill and W. Clement Stone
Recommended by: Jerry Heffel, President, The Southwestern Company

Along with people, books are an important part of my life; and there are many which have been influential. Next to the Bible, one in particular stands out in my mind.

Perhaps the timing was right. I was a young college student contemplating the many directions my life could take in terms of a career. The Southwestern Company gave me an opportunity to take part in their summer sales program. It was there that I received a copy of *Success through a Positive Mental Attitude*. Its impact upon my thinking was dramatic.

Looking back over the years, it is very apparent to me how significantly my thinking has been shaped by the principles Napoleon Hill and Clement Stone shared with me through their book. For one thing, it crystallized in printed form many of the values instilled in me by my family. Second of all, the philosophies this book teaches draw heavily from the greatest book of all–God's Word.

It is a book which gives the "why" and the "how." It motivates people to act! It is highly readable and well organized. Each chapter concludes with a key statement, and "Thoughts To Steer By." The following are a few which have stuck with me over the past 20 years:

"Success is achieved and maintained by those who keep trying." . . . "Anything in life worth having is worth working for!" . . . "You can do it if you believe you can!" . . . "That which you share will multiply and that which you withhold will diminish!"

The Act of Will

by Roberto Assagioli, M.D.
Recommended by: Christopher J. Hegarty, CPAE,
President, Christopher J. Hegarty and Company

The reason I am so taken by *The Act of Will*, by Roberto Assagioli, M.D., is that it has a step-by-step blueprint for how we can begin to direct our Will in a creative, integrated way rather than attempt to make severe demands of positive thinking.

Assagioli practiced, applied and enlightened psychology for more than fifty years. Headquartered in Florence, Italy, he founded the school of psychology called psychosynthesis. Without exception, every practitioner I have met who is familiar with psychosynthesis finds it valuable, some calling it the most important work on psychology and human behavior they have ever known. Chapter Five, "The Skillful Will: Psychological Laws," is the most important chapter in the book. It shows a series of understandable steps to take to integrate our thinking with our imagination, our emotions, our impulses, and thereby direct our Will.

The Magic of Self Direction

by David J. Schwartz, Ph.D.
Recommended by: Bob Henry, C.P.A.E.,
Past Pres., National Speakers Association

This book tells you how to get the most out of life by controlling your mind.

The secret to success lies in your ability to purposefully manipulate your thoughts so that winning not only becomes possible but inevitable. Whatever you want in life is available to you – wealth, success, friends, freedom from fear and worry, power, material and spiritual rewards – if you will learn to consistently think in a powerful, positive, forceful way.

Dr. Schwartz gives programs for mental computers. This book is loaded with mental exercises which aid one in joining the winning team. You'll learn how to break the bonds of psychological slavery, use psychic power to gain help from others, stop worrying and start living, gain courage and overcome fear, get ahead by thinking bigger, let your brain make you rich, use mental power to dominate and control others and much more.

The author emphatically believes that success and happiness is a matter of conscious choice. He gives you the tools, simply stated, to make the right choices.

David Schwartz is a wonderful writer. His style is simple, clear and conversational. Some of his ideas and examples you may have heard before, yet the truisms don't change and he presents them in an easily accepted format.

The Greatest Secret in the World

by Og Mandino
Recommended by: Les Hewitt,
President & Founder, Achievers Canada

Og Mandino's wonderful book, *The Greatest Secret in the World*, has had a major impact on my thinking. Success in any form is simply a matter of discipline. The ten scrolls challenge you to a daily discipline that forces a new imprint on your mental awareness. Here are a few examples that helped me:

"I will form good habits and become their slave."

"I will welcome obstacles for they are my challenge."

"I will persist until I succeed."

"Procrastination I will destroy with action."

"Today I will be master of my emotions."

"So long as I can laugh never will I be poor."

The magic of Og Mandino's book is the discipline you are forced to endure in order to read the scrolls three times a day. That alone is well worth the time. An added bonus are the pearls of wisdom buried within the scrolls for you to discover and use.

International Executives

When the Going Gets Tough

by Billy Burden
Recommended by: Dr. Oskar Pack,
Professional Speaker, West Germany

There have been several books which meant very much to me in the various parts of my life. But there is one which became of special help and special value to me, because it helped me in a very critical and difficult situation of my life.

I kept *When the Going Gets Tough* permanently with me in my briefcase. I did not read it, but I studied it. When driving along the Autobahn, I parked in places and read from it. I knew personally several individuals whose struggles against difficult situations it described: Dave Yoho, Marguerite Piazza, Art Linkletter, Earl Nightingale. What Dr. Norman Vincent Peale says on the cover "A book that will give you fresh courage, wise insights and a restored faith in your own ability to overcome any problem," this is true. This book has been of tremendous help to me in my own situation. Therefore I am recommending it highly.

You Can Become the Person You Want to Be

by Robert Schuller
Recommended by: Lee David,
Executive, Northern Ireland

See You at the Top

by Zig Ziglar
Recommended by: David Goh,
Professional Speaker, Malaysia

To the question of a book that has changed my lifestyle and helped me to become better, it is Zig Ziglar's *See You at the Top*. This book taught me to think.

International Executives

Think and Grow Rich

by Napoleon Hill
Recommended by: Lawrence Chan Kum Peng, Pres., Personal Development Leadership Management Corporation—Malaysia

The book that has really made me think very seriously about my life is *Think and Grow Rich*, which I read in December, 1971. Since then, as a Trainer, I have personally sold more than 10,000 copies of this book to the participants in my seminars.

Why We Act Like Canadians

Leland Val Vandewall, President, Xoces—Canada

Think and Grow Rich

by Napoleon Hill
Recommended by: Terry Bilham, Insurance Executive, England

The very first book I ever read which started me off on this power packed career was *Think and Grow Rich*. Here are a few choice thoughts:

"You have absolute control over but one thing, and that is your thoughts. This is the most significant and inspiring of all-facts known to man! It reflects man's divine nature. This divine prerogative is the sole means by which you may control your own destiny. If you fail to control your own mind, you may be sure you will control nothing else. If you must be careless with your possessions, let it be in connection with material things. *Your mind is your spiritual estate!* Protect and use it with the care to which divine royalty is entitled. You were given a will-power for this purpose."

Creating a Success Environment

by Keith DeGreen
Recommended by: Roger Himes, Attorney, Professional Speaker, Author

Being a lawyer, I know people love living by rules and laws. We love a rule book because we like knowing whether we're right or wrong, and a rule book helps us stay in bounds – it gives us a certain framework to operate in. Therefore, we love success books that guarantee us the 3, 7, 10, or 15½ easy steps to success. This way we can "get it down" in our heads so we know the principles. However, they seldom succeed in helping us plant their concepts the 18 inches lower necessary to reach our hearts.

Keith's book doesn't take this approach. It looks at every facet of life for a complete, well-rounded, balanced life-style. It's clear that success doesn't depend on whether you're only walking toward the mountain, or have reached the mountaintop. Rather, success is determined by the direction in which you're going – in all areas of life. Remember, you won't have a very successful, safe trip if you're trying to drive with one or more flat tires! Just having your life running well in one area doesn't cut the mustard.

Plus, Keith gives us a very helpful formula by which to measure our growth. The formula, $SE - (I \times O \times H \times W) Y$, takes into consideration our thinking, attitudes, emotions, logic, appearance, health, marriage, family, work, relationships, money, goals, and other things. It then takes into consideration the extent to which we control and manage our growth in any and all areas of life on a weekly, monthly, or annual basis.

The Greatest Salesman in the World

by Og Mandino
Recommended by: Tom Hopkins
President, Tom Hopkins International

It's a quandary for me to choose one book out of my library that had the greatest impact on my life. I do believe, however, that I must choose *The Greatest Salesman in the World* by Og Mandino. Many years ago, this book greatly helped me with my attitude and self-image change. The impact was so great on me because of the "storybook" format built with tremendous psychological truths of happiness and achievement. If a person dedicated themselves to live by the 10 scrolls and follow the assignments, they would have a definite change in their emotional stability take place.

As in any book that asks for time and home study commitment, if a person lacks the discipline to make the time to go through the exercises they truly are wasting the time they have spent reading the material. So many people want to change their environment and experience a greater degree of success and dine on the delicacies of our society, however, they keep looking outside of themselves for the answers instead of realizing the only thing holding him back is between his ears. If a person can alter the thinking process and fill their minds with knowledge, they can then have a truly positive impact in changing their lifestyle and outlook on life.

Many people say, "oh, if I was rich I would be enthusiastic, too." I am finding those people that are rich emotionally, physically, financially and spiritually radiate their aura of enthusiasm before the riches become theirs. We are all trying to change someone, but must realize that any long lasting change must come from that person.

The Healing of Persons

by Paul Tournier
Recommended by: T. Willard Hunter, Professional Speaker

Moving up fast in the worlds of therapy is "holistic" medicine. Norman Cousins, among others, has popularized the concept of involving the whole person in healing. Ever since World War II, however, the most consistent popular writer in the field has been a Swiss doctor, Paul Tournier. His 16 books have shared with a vast, global audience the effectiveness of the psychological and spiritual healing he has brought to his patients.

Biographers say the turning point in Tournier's life, as well as his whole approach to medicine, came at 34 when he met some people of the World Renewal Movement in Geneva in 1932. The restorative impetus of this group, which was later called Moral Re-Armament, was in the thirties to generate Alcoholics Anonymous and a long line of derivatives.

Key thoughts in *The Healing of Persons*.

1. Life is "an adventure of living, led by God."
2. Since man "is a unity: body, mind, and spirit," treatment is to be done "in the person's entirety."
3. The "unscientific" and "materialistic" assumption is false "that material facts are the cause and that moral facts are the consequence, and not the other way around."

Legion are Dr. Tournier's "patients" whom he has never seen, but whose lives have been changed through his books. And this ripple effect will never end.

Maximum Life Span

by Dr. Roy L. Walford
Recommended by: Don Hutson, CPAE,
Certified Speaking Professional

As one who has been a student of longevity and the aging process for many years, I was very positively impacted by this work by Dr. Roy L. Walford. We are at the dawn of a new era in health consciousness and this enormously factual and thought-provoking book puts many things in proper perspective for us.

Dr. Walford presents an interesting and convincing premise that science is now on the brink of life-extension breakthroughs that will soon enable us to live to 120 years and more. I find it amusing that the majority of us have assumed for the most part that we will live a "normal" life into our seventies and eighties, then fade away into the hereafter on schedule. If Roy Walford's prophecies materialize, we'll have more frustrated actuaries at insurance companies and social security analysts in Washington than one could believe. We will probably also have some expectant heirs beside themselves!

This book helps you understand a person's allotted span of life is simply too short to permit a satisfying exploration of the world's outer wonders and the realms of inner experience. We are cut off in the midst of our pleasures, separated too soon from our loved ones, shelved at the mere beginning of our understanding.

How to Live 365 Days a Year

by Dr. John A. Schindler, M.D.
Recommended by: Charles W. Jarvis, DD. CPAE

Years ago, Dr. Schindler's book made me aware of my emotions, that either I can control them, or they will control me. He made me aware of what I now try to get across with my humor, that we are responsible for our success and our happiness, and that we must have BALANCE in our lives as a goal. His discussion of equanimity and emotional status is very enlightening and necessary to the happy and successful individual.

"PRESCRIPTION FOR THE HAPPY LIFE"–my first talk, which has been given hundreds of times in this country and Canada, had my thoughts piggy-backed with those of this doctor of much common sense, Dr. Schindler. He helped me, and through me, has helped (I hope) thousands of others.

There are not many people in the world who can make folks feel better for having had their lives touch others. I try to be one of those, and judge my success that way and by the BALANCE in my own personal life. A dental colleague once told me, "Charlie, we can all do dentistry, but we cannot all make people laugh. If you ever quit one or the other, I hope you will quit dentistry." I laughingly replied, "You've seen my dentistry, haven't you?" "Yes," he grinned, "but I think you render a better service making people laugh than you could in dentistry."

Get this book, study it, and your life will change. Yes, for the better.

Tough Minded Optimist

by Norman Vincent Peale
Recommended by: Paul R. Jeffers, CLU,
President, Paul R. Jeffers, Inc.

I read all the time and it would be very, very difficult to say which book is my favorite, since there are so many that are extremely good. If I had to pick one, it would have to be Norman Vincent Peale's *Tough Minded Optimist*.

I think the thing that I would have to say about it, is that I believe strongly that we can't get along in this world unless we're positive thinkers. We have much going for us if we think positively, and nothing going for us if we're negative. I think that Norman Vincent Peale's books point this out extremely well. I believe everybody in the United States should read them and read them more than once. I feel that next to the Bible, this is one of the greatest books ever written.

Norman Vincent Peale has a way of making people think about what they should be doing. I would highly recommend this book to anyone.

The diffusion of these silent teachers, – books – through the whole community is to work greater effects than artillery, machinery, and legislation. Its peaceful agency is to supersede stormy revolutions. The culture which it is to spread, whilst an unspeakable good to the individual, is also to become the stability of nations.

– Channing

The Velveteen Rabbit

by Marjorie Williams
Recommended by: James N. Jeffrey, Director, Financial Development, American Red Cross

The book that I could recommend to others is *The Velveteen Rabbit*, by Marjorie Williams. The book is about one of the essential ingredients in life needed if we are to approach our full potential. It deals with becoming REAL in the fullest sense of the word, as in being honest, believable, and trustworthy, etc.

The book is about a toy velveteen rabbit stuffed with sawdust who has a desire to become real and seeks the advice of a toy skin horse who has become a sage because of his longevity. The Rabbit finds out that being real isn't how you are made, rather, it is something that happens to you. "Generally, by the time you are real, most of your hair has been loved off, and your eyes drop out and you get loose in the joints and very shabby. But, those things don't matter at all because once you are real, you can't be ugly, except to people who don't understand."

The love of the little boy who owned the velveteen rabbit made him real and he was happy to learn that, "once you are real you can't become unreal again. It lasts for always."

The book goes on to describe many meaningful things that parallel real life. I believe that the heavenly Father is the only one that can make us real. He has the power not only to forgive us but to sustain us throughout our lifetime. Not because of our goodness or our prestige or our many talents and resources, but because of our faith in Him. This little book, *The Velveteen Rabbit*, has been an inspiration to me. I recommend it.

The Book

The Book First

Recommended by: George C. Lorimer
1896

I have no doubt that the Apostle Paul, when he exhorted Timothy to "give attendance to reading," had special and perhaps exclusive reference to the reading of the Scriptures. This is the view of the most eminent critics, and I see no reason for questioning its soundness. Above and before all other writings ought the Bible be prized. Viewed simply as literature its claims are paramount; such a composition, for instance, as that of "Job" surpassing in genuine poetic spirit that of "Faust," while the magnificent flights of eloquence that fill the pages of "Isaiah" are unmatched by Wordsworth; and not even Browning, though in some respects suggesting his dramatic and metaphysical style, can compare with Jeremiah in loftiness of thought and grandeur of expression.

That Bible whose composition appealed to the refined taste of Matthew Arnold; that Bible whose dignity and sublimity aroused the soul of Heine so that he regarded the volume as a breath of paradise; that Bible whose prose the skeptical Frederic Harrison extols so highly; that Bible which George Eliot read daily at Witely, and which was to him a very precious and sacred book; yea, the Bible which even Diderot, while rejecting, commended to his child as her best guide in morals and purity.

Every Great Book from Bible

by Clyde W. Taylor

So closely is the Bible allied with the literature of the world that DeWitt Talmage said:

"Every great book that has been published since the first printing press has directly or indirectly derived much of its power from the Sacred Oracles.

"Milton's *Paradise Lost* is borrowed from the Bible; Spencer's writings are imitations of the parables; John Bunyan saw in a dream what Saint John had previously seen in a vision; Macauley crowns his most gigantic sentences with Scripture quotations.

"Walter Scott's characters are Bible men and women under different names; Hobbs stole from this Castle of Truth the weapons with which he afterward attacked it; and the writings of Pope are saturated with Isaiah. The Bible is the fountain of truth from which other good books dip their life."

The Book

It ain't those parts of the Bible that I can't understand that bother me, it is the parts that I do understand.

–Mark Twain

We call upon the German people once again: "Guard what you have!" Let no man rob you of your priceless . . . sacred books!

–Faulhaber 1935

The Jews were the only ones whose sacred Scriptures were held in ever greater veneration as they became better known.

–Bossuet 1681

It is precisely in the Old Testament that is reached the highest ethical note ever yet sounded . . . by man.

–Zangwill 1918

The Bible . . . is the classical book of noble ethical sentiment. In it the mortal fear, the overflowing hope, the quivering longings of the human soul . . . have found their first, their freshest, their fittest utterance.

–F. Adler 1877

Almost any fool can prove that the Bible ain't so–it takes a wise man to believe it.

–Josh Billings

The Book

The Bible tells us to love our neighbors, and also to love our enemies; probably because they are generally the same people.

–G. K. Chesterton

What is the Bible in your house? It is not the Old Testament, it is not the New Testament, it is not the Gospel according to Matthew or Mark, or Luke or John; it is the Gospel according to William, it is the Gospel according to Mary, it is the Gospel according to Henry and James, it is the Gospel according to your name. You write your own Bible.

–Beecher

The Bible is a warm letter of affection from a parent to a child; and yet there are many who see chiefly the severer passages. As there may be fifty or sixty nights of gentle dews in one summer, that will not cause as much remark as one hailstorm of half an hour, so there are those who are more struck by those passages of the Bible that announce the indignation of God than by those that announce His affection.

–T. DeWitt Talmage

The Bible is a book of faith, and a book of doctrine, and a book of morals, and a book of religion, of special revelation from God; but it is also a book which teaches man his own individual responsibility, his own dignity, and his equality with his fellow man.

–Daniel Webster

Wilbur M. Smith and The Book

Well, you are about to enter upon a thrilling experience. You will find the study of the Scriptures the most exhilarating, fascinating and satisfying work you have ever undertaken. The Bible is inexhaustible, and has had more written about it, of course, than has been written about the twenty greatest classics of world literature combined – and we have still not exhausted its wealth. Its truths are forever settled in heaven; its prophecies mold the destinies of nations; as the water of life, it cleanses our souls; as a seed, it imparts life; as bread, it nourishes us; and the entrance of the Word into our hearts delivers us from darkness and fear. May the Spirit of God Himself take the things of Christ and reveal them unto you both day by day, and page by page.

How much there is to know in this world that we shall never know! But how much richer life can become by a steady application, if only thirty minutes a day, to the study of some noble subject relating to the Christian faith.

Book of Books

by J. C. Penney

There may be those who say they have lost, if they ever had it, the faculty for study. They tell us they find no fascination in books. We grant such a deplorable condition possible, but what then? Why not cultivate a taste for study? Why not seek to re-acquire a fondness for those things which study alone assures? Why not try to learn how to appreciate the joys that result from mental effort? The time spent in the pursuit of knowledge and understanding is rewarded by a realization of ideals and a growth in power and determination.

Books readily or easily understood are seldom worth the time consumed in reading them. Cultivate a taste for the Good, the Better, the Best – the most profitable study. "The finest reading is in the Book of Books."

D. L. Moody and Spurgeon's Bible

The following were entries made in the Bible given to D. L. Moody by Mrs. Spurgeon:

"C. H. Spurgeon.
"The lamp of my study. 1858.
"The light is as bright as ever. 1861
"Oh that mine eyes were more opened! 1864.
"Being worn to pieces, rebound 1870. The lantern mended and the light as joyous to mine eyes as ever."

Presidents and the Book

"Inside the Bible's pages lie all the answers to all the problems man has ever known. I hope Americans will read and study the Bible. . . . It is my firm belief that the enduring values presented in its pages have a great meaning for each of us and for our nation. The Bible can touch our hearts, order our minds, and refresh our souls."

–Ronald Reagan

The Bible is the rock on which the Republic rests.

–Andrew Jackson

Almost every man who has by his life-work added to the sum of human achievement, of which the world is proud–almost every such man has based his life-work upon the teaching of the Bible.

–Theodore Roosevelt

The first and almost the only book deserving of universal attention is the Bible. I speak as a man of the world to men of the world, and I say to you, "Search the Scriptures". . . . The earlier my children begin to read it the more confident will be my hopes that they will prove useful citizens of their country and respectable members of society.

–John Quincy Adams

"I believe the Bible is the best gift God has ever given to man. All the good from the Savior of the world is communicated to us through this book."

–Abraham Lincoln

The Book of Books

How many ages and generations have brooded and wept and agonized over this book! What untellable joys and ecstasies, what support to martyrs at the stake from it! To what myriads has it been the shore and rock of safety–the refuge from driving tempest and wreck! Translated in all languages, how it has united the diverse world!

–Walt Whitman

The circulation of the Holy Scriptures has done more, perhaps, than anything else on earth to promote moral and religious welfare among old and young.

–King George V

Today man sees all his hopes and aspirations crumbling before him. He is perplexed and knows not whither he is drifting. But he must realize that the Bible is his refuge and the rallying point for all humanity. In it man will find the solution of his present difficulties and guidance for his future action, and unless he accepts with clear conscience the Bible and its great message, he cannot hope for salvation. For my part, I glory in the Bible.

–Haile Selassie
Emperor of Ethiopia

Great Americans and the Book

The Bible is worth all the other books which have ever been printed.

–Patrick Henry

If we abide by the principles taught in the Bible, our country will go on prospering and to prosper; but if we and our posterity neglect its instructions and authority, no man can tell how sudden a catastrophe may overwhelm us and bury our glory in profound obscurity.

–Daniel Webster

It is impossible to enslave mentally or socially a Bible-reading people. The principles of the Bible are the groundwork of human freedom.

–Horace Greeley

The Bible is a book in comparison with which all others in my eyes are of minor importance; and which in all my perplexities and distresses has never failed to give me light and strength.

–Robert E. Lee

Woodrow Wilson and the Book

The Bible is the Word of Life. I beg you will read it and find this out for yourself – read, not little snatches here and there, but long passages that will really be the road to the heart of it.

You will not only find it full of real men and women, but also of things you have wondered about and been troubled about all your life, as men have been always, and the more you read, the more will it become plain to you what things are worthwhile and what are not; what things make men happy – loyalty, right dealing, speaking the truth, readiness to give everything for what they think their duty, and, most of all, the wish that they may have the real approval of the Christ, who gave everything for them; and the things that are guaranteed to make men unhappy – selfishness, cowardice, greed, and everything that is low and mean.

When you have read the Bible, you will know that it is the Word of God, because you will have found it the key to your own heart, your own happiness, and your own duty.

Field-Marshal Montgomery and the Book

Known to his soldiers as "Monty," and possessing a curious blend of ruthlessness and tenderness in his personality, Montgomery has become known throughout the world as one of the greatest generals of modern times. And yet, it is not an uncommon sight to see him standing bareheaded in the field conducting divine services.

No man has captured the fancy and admiration of the military and civilian world like the hero of El Alamein. An individualist, "Monty" possesses rare military acumen and a powerful personality. Known as a strict disciplinarian, greatly concerned about details, and a zealous exponent of physical fitness, he nonetheless possesses the admiration and the love of his soldiers.

His victories have been achieved with a Bible in one hand and a dog-eared copy of *Pilgrim's Progress* in the other. His much-used Bible is never far from him. Constantly he tells his men, "I read at least one chapter in the Bible every day, and I recommend that you do the same." His military reports often include verses from Scripture; messages to his troops frequently contain passages from The Book which is exceedingly precious to him.

T. De Witt Talmage and the Book

This book is the hive of all sweetness, the armory of all well-tempered weapons, the tower containing the crown jewels of the universe, the lamp that kindles all other lights, the home of all majesties and splendors, the stepping-stone on which heaven stoops to kiss the earth with its glories, the marriage-ring that unites the celestial and the terrestrial, while all the clustering white-robed multitudes of the sky stand round to rejoice at the nuptials. This book is the wreath into which are twisted all garlands, the song into which hath struck all harmonies, the river of light into which hath poured all the great tides of hallelujahs, the firmament in which all suns and moons and stars and constellations and galaxies and immensities and universes and eternities wheel and blaze and triumph.

D. L. Moody and the Book

He nourished and strengthened his life by devotion to God's Word. He prized it as the treasure by which his life could be enriched. He realised to the full Christ's words, "Man shall not live by bread alone, but by every word that proceedeth out of the mouth of God." That Word he hid in his heart, as the seed is hidden in the earth that it may swell and grow. He hid it there, ready for use on every occasion and in every emergency. It was sweeter to him than honey and the honeycomb. His mind and heart were given to the Word of God.

"But his life, like that of Christ, was for others. He did not search the Bible to add to his knowledge, but to save men from sin."

Moses Mendelssohn and the Book

As a child Moses lacked neither the will nor the capacity for study. One of his early teachers, named Hirsch, whose father was a member of the Beth Din (rabbinic court) of Dessau, testified in later years to the piety, zeal, and the brightness of the lad. Euchel reports that at the age of six Moses had already begun to study "Halakha and Tosafot," i.e. the Talmud with its commentaries and the codes. The correctness of this statement need not be doubted. The teaching method prevalent in the *Heder* or Beth Hamidrash aimed at familiarity with the Talmud and neglected the Bible and its classical commentaries. Even as a child, however, Moses showed a degree of independence: he loved to read the Bible on his own and became so well versed in it that he came to know large portions of the Hebrew text by heart. He also studied Hebrew grammar and strove to gain facility in writing Hebrew prose and poetry in the biblical style. He is said to have tried his hand at the writing of poetry at the age of ten but to have soon realized his lack of talent in that respect. How successful he was in his linguistic exercises was to manifest itself later in his extensive literary output in Hebrew, which excels in both beauty and precision. One may say that already as a child he showed himself imbued with the love of classical Hebrew that was to become one of the distinctive features of the Haskala, the early phase of the Jewish Enlightenment in Germany. By the same token, the fondness for the Bible and for biblical studies, which lead him to his German translations of the Hebrew texts of the Psalms, Canticles, and above all the Pentateuch, goes back to the strong attachment to the Bible that he developed as a child.

A Book I'd Like To Share

Growing Strong in the Seasons of Life

by Charles R. Swindoll
Recommended by: Don Johnson, President, Herrick Corporation

Dr. Swindoll's book was the most profitable one I read in 1984. Containing short inspirational and practical essays on many of the realities of life and how we can cope with them, *Growing Strong in the Seasons of Life* is an outstandng guide to applied Christianity. It is an action book which demands a response to its challenges.

Typical of the salty subjects discussed are consistency, disillusionment, back to the basics, fear, presumption, isolation, involvement, resentment, rationalization, plus many more. Written in a direct but warm conversational style, this book has been like a close personal friend in challenging and encouraging me to live life to its intended limits.

"THERE'S NO NEED TO TAKE GOD SERIOUSLY."

"I know of no philosophy more popular today. It's the reason we're caught these days in the do-your-own-thing *sin*drome. What a subtle web the spider of self has woven! Millions are stuck – and instead of screaming, 'I'm caught!' they shout, with a smile, 'I'm free!'

"If you don't take God seriously, then there's no need to take your marriage seriously . . . or the rearing of children . . . or such character traits as submission, faithfulness, sexual purity, humility, repentance, and honesty."

Samuel Johnson and Books

The particular course of his reading while at Oxford, and during the time of vacation which he passed at home, cannot be traced. Enough has been said of his irregular mode of study. He told me, that from his earliest years he loved to read poetry, but hardly ever read any poem to an end; that he read Shakespeare at a period so early, that the speech of the Ghost in Hamlet terrified him when he was alone; that Horace's Odes were the compositions in which he took most delight, and it was long before he liked his Epistles and Satires. He told me what he read solidly at Oxford was Greek; not the Grecian historians, but Homer and Euripides, and now and then a little Epigram; that the study of which he was most fond was Metaphysicks, but he had not read much, even in that way. I always thought that he did himself injustice in his account of what he had read, and that he must have been speaking with reference to the vast portion of study which is possible, and to which a few scholars in the world history of literature have attained. Dr. Adam Smith, than whom few were better judges on this subject, once observed to me that "Johnson knew more books than any man alive."

–Boswell

Winning Strategies in Selling

by Jack Kinder, Jr., Garry Kinder, Roger Staubach
Recommended by: Mary Jones, Sales Consultant, Mary Jones & Associates

I discovered this book to be a "college-type" textbook on selling. It's simple. It's easy to understand. It's must reading for anyone striving for professionalism in selling.

This book is packed with dozens of full worked-out strategies used by many of the best and highest paid sales pros in the country, i.e. Mary Kay Ash of Mary Kay Cosmetics; Rich DeVos, President of Amway; and some of the nation's top authorities on competitiveness, drive and fitness, such as Dr. Kenneth Cooper, of the Aerobic Center and Dr. Denis Waitley.

This "how-to" book reveals such effective sales techniques as the all-important methods of gaining instant attention from prospects using "plus benefits" and "minus benefits"; unusual new strategies for staying in total control of the prospect and sales process; and simple follow-up tactics that will get readers satisfied customers and repeat business.

I agree with Earl Nightingale when he says: "if you never had the opportunity to read another book on how to sell, you would find *Winning Strategies in Selling* to be quite sufficient."

See You at the Top

by Zig Ziglar
Recommended by: Mike Kafka, Executive Vice President, Bel Kraft International Ltd.

Zig Ziglar's book, *See You at the Top*, has taught me there is NO instant success. As Zig says, "The Elevator To The Top Is Out Of Order!":

"For many people, *See You at the Top* has been the road map to greater accomplishment and this simple formula has been the catalyst that started them. It could well be the catalyst you seek but I must warn you, there is a certain danger involved in following the formula. When you buy the ideas, adopt the attitude and follow the procedures I recommend, you'll encounter some interesting reactions. Some will criticize you and say you're different, and of course they'll be right. You'll be so different you'll be one of the few people in the game of life who will be able to open life's vault of valuables and get what you want instead of having to want what you have. For what it's worth, I wouldn't be overly concerned about the critics. Since the beginning of recorded history, no one has erected a statue to a critic. So, they must not be held in too much esteem."

Just as important as the content of his book, is the fact that it's easily understood by most people that I have recommended it to.

Professional Speakers

Journey

by Robert and Susie Massie
Recommended by: Danielle Kennedy

One of my all-time favorite inspirational books is *Journey*, by a husband and wife, Robert and Susie Massie.

Journey is the story of a boy and his family's stretch to greatness. The son is a hemophilliac and the drama of his journey to adolescence, along with his parents' struggle to help him, was inspiring.

I particularly loved it because of the tremendous feeling of gratefulness and appreciation I have for my family and the respect for life this book reminds us all of – we take breath, blood and life for granted.

The Ultimate Secret

by Mike Hernaki
Recommended by: Lee Shapiro

The Inner Game of Tennis

by Timothy Gallway
Recommended by: Hank Trisler

This was particularly beneficial to me, as Gallway provides easily used drills and exercises designed to prevent the conscious mind from overriding the inherent excellence of the unconscious mind.

Our unconscious minds are capable of truly amazing execution of complex tasks, if the constant carping of the highly judgmental conscious mind can be stilled. Just look at the skilled muscular motions required to brush our teeth, or walk down stairs, yet we all do this daily with absolutely no input required from the conscious mind.

Gallway's methods are useful not only for tennis, but for golf, selling and, yes, for all facets of daily living. I highly recommend it.

The Secrets of Closing

by Charles B. Roth
Recommended by: Jack Kinder, Jr.,
Sales and Management Consultant

The ability to close sales is still the most important dimension in any successful salesperson's life. To be sure, there are a myriad of new products and services that salespeople are selling today–all the way from satellite communication systems to computer software packages, and, yes, to future bookings for space trips to the moon. The principles by which these new wonder products and services are purveyed, are the age old principles of salesmanship which are effectively developed by Charles Roth in this book.

The rich storehouse of ideas and principles found in this book have formed the basis of the closing strategies we teach in our consulting practice. It's the single finest book on the closing process we have ever read and studied.

You're ambitious to make the most of every selling day. You want to earn more money. You want to climb in the selling profession. You want to become a salesperson who closes sales that don't close themselves.

The Secrets of Closing will show you how to realize each of these desires. Read and inwardly digest this book. Live with it. Take it to heart. It will move you into the big league in selling.

The Magic of Thinking Big

by Dr. David J. Schwartz
Recommended by: Kirk Kirkpatrick, Professional Speaker, Publisher of Quote *Magazine*

Luckily for me, a few years ago I purchased *The Magic of Thinking Big*. At the risk of overstatement, THINKING BIG changed my life.

It came at a time when it seemed that I had about reached my peak in my career. Any success I've enjoyed since then, at least in part, has come from reading and, yes, rereading this marvelous book. Since that time, I've worked with the author, Dr. David J. Schwartz. He truly is a Big Thinker. Not only does he THINK BIG . . . he gets big results. This is important to me. He practices what he preaches.

Not only has THINKING BIG helped me tremendously, it has become a success method for millions of people worldwide. These people now look for the optimum in all phases of their lives and careers. They have learned to think big, plan big, and execute in a big way.

There have been advertising themes, sales campaigns, and corporate game plans created around this solid, workable theme. There is a big reason . . . it works. No wonder it has gone through its 35th printing by Prentice Hall.

THINKING BIG has also been used in education, religion, and in many other activities where a rallying theme is needed. Once a person or a group adopts this as a plan for self-motivation, they never fail to keep this plan uppermost in their minds. Nothing can change their vision. They continue upward and forward . . . THINKING BIG.

New Think

by Edward de Bono
Recommended by: M. R. Kopmeyer, Author, President, The Success Foundation

When I asked a group of top business leaders what books they were reading, the consensus was *New Think, The Next American Frontier*, and *In Search of Excellence*. I, too, have read these three excellent business books and I would like to comment here on *New Think*.

New Think was written by Edward de Bono and published in 1967. So *New Think* is not new, but that does not make it less effective. The title of the book is simply a clever name for what is better known as lateral thinking, which was well known before Edward de Bono wrote his pleasant and intelligent little book about it.

Actually, there are four kinds of thinking: Vertical thinking, Lateral thinking, Alternative thinking, and Jigsaw Puzzle thinking.

The book *New Think* emphasizes lateral thinking over the more widely used vertical thinking for problem solving. It describes vertical thinking as being like digging one hole in the ground, and continuing to dig deeper and deeper in the same hole even though the problem is not solved.

New Think admonishes, "Go dig someplace else, many places else!" Lateral thinking. Testing the full range of possible solutions until the successful solution is found. I agree.

Alcoholics Anonymous

Recommended by: Harry Ladd,
Certified Speaking Professional

I have read many books that have influenced my life, some more than others. Without a doubt, the GREATEST BOOK I have ever read is *Alcoholics Anonymous*. It has had 48 printings since its first publication in 1939.

The contents of this book would APPLY TO ANYONE, not just recovering alcoholics.

Alcoholics Anonymous is the "set of directions" that have helped the most people recover from an incurable disease. Although the book has 575 pages, the FIRST 164 are the most important. They list 12 simple steps to follow for a more spiritual life. The contents place STRONG EMPHASIS on the fact that living a happy life is based on one's SPIRITUAL RELATIONSHIP with a Higher Power. The reader is given his OWN CHOICE of that Higher Power, whether it be God, Jesus, or whoever else is chosen. The important thing is: establish that relationship.

The 12 Steps are simple. The results are guaranteed if the directions are followed.

Pages 83 and 84 of the book list the "promises"–that which will happen if the steps are followed. It is absolutely incredible how this simple program works! Any person who has followed the steps will attest to the fact that the "promises" do happen.

Love Is Letting Go of Fear

by Gerald G. Jampolsky
Recommended by: Robert Larsen,
Insurance Executive

In a very poetic and simple way, Jerry Jampolsky demonstrates the art of letting go of fear. He talks about a change in perspective, a change in view, and he allows you to walk with him through a series of simple situations which will help you see how silly it is to constrict yourself with fear and to ruin the days you have here on Earth. He shows how your fear can cause fear in others. He shows how your fear brings you to fearful situations and how silly it is to do the thing to yourself that is exactly opposite to what you want. He clarifies love and lets you know the strongest energy on Earth is that God-given emotion, that feeling of love we have to give to ourselves and all those around us.

Love is the only way in which we can eliminate this insidious disease of fearful thinking. Learning how to get what you really want out of life, is learning how to love. Spread it and spill it all around. Try to see yourself as a gift to give. Try giving a smile away. Try reminding someone when they are acting terribly to the people around them, that they are better than that and that God loves them. They were created in love and love does no harm to the world around it. Love heals and warms the environment. Love takes away the pain and fills the heart with joy.

D. H. Lawrence and Books

Lawrence's mother had a taste of books, so that from childhood he was accustomed to seeing them as an accepted part of life. She and the children belonged to the Literary Society attached to the Congregationalist Church.

Jessie Chambers kept a list of the authors she and Lawrence read together. She mentions more than a hundred authors nearly all English and French and of the nineteenth century. Their chief source was Palgrave's *Golden Treasury*, which Lawrence at one time always carried and enjoyed reading aloud. Along with the *Treasury* they read Scott, Tennyson, Swinburne, Whitman, Rossetti, Browning and Francis Thompson. At some time during his student life he read parts of Horace and Virgil in the original as well as Baudelaire and Verlaine, whom he greatly admired. In one of his *Assorted Articles* he speaks of the "lovely poems which after all give the ultimate shape to one's life – The Odes of Keats and Wordsworth, parts of Shakespeare, Goethe's lyrics, Verlaine." He read many other books even in those days and read extensively when he was at Croydon.

The novel is the highest example of subtle interrelatedness that man has discovered.

–D. H. Lawrence

The Lessons of History

by Will and Ariel Durant
Recommended by: John Lee, CPAE,
President, John Lee Companies

I first read Will and Ariel Durant's *The Lessons of History* in 1969 and used this text as a required reading in my Great Management Books programs at Florida State University for six years. At the end of every program, the Durants' short 101-page text ranked number one in discussion and insights. Every time I re-read it I also discover new relationships and explanations to current problems that only history can provide.

While the Durants are best known for their lifetime work on their 10-volume *Story of Civilization*, more people have read and benefited from *The Lessons of History*. You can't judge a book by its cover, but you can by its authors. Few historians come close to the Durants in terms of their contribution and optimism for the future. "The present is the past rolled up for action and the past is the present unrolled for understanding," noted the Durants. And so must we if we are to make intelligent decisions about our futures.

The Sky Pilot

by Ralph Conner

From Robert G. Lee, The Authorized Biography *by John E. Huss*

Early in life Bob displayed a passion for books. There was one special book, in addition to the Bible, which had a powerful influence on his formative years in molding his thoughts concerning the ministry. The name of the book was *The Sky Pilot*, authored by Ralph Conner, the pen name under which Dr. Charles W. Gordon wrote his many books. This book was given to him, when he was fifteen years old, by a young woman who expressed the wish that someday Lee might become a minister and do for people what the Sky Pilot did for those with whom he lived.

The Sky Pilot tells of the people of the California Foothill Country; of those men of adventurous spirit who left homes of comfort because of the stirring in them to be and to do the worthy thing. It tells of others who, outcast from their kind, sought to find in the valleys a spot where they could forget and be forgotten. To these people came the Sky Pilot. He came to them with a firm purpose to play the brother's part. By sheer love for them and by faith in them, he caused them to believe that life is priceless.

Later in life, after rereading the book many times, Lee traveled more than a hundred miles to meet its author and express warm thanks for the message of the book.

C. S. Lewis and The Lord of the Rings

This book is like lightning from a clear sky; as sharply different, as unpredictable in our age as *Songs of Innocence* were in theirs. To say that in it heroic romance, gorgeous, eloquent, and unashamed, has suddenly returned at a period almost pathological in its anti-romanticism is inadequate. To us, who live in that odd period, the return–and the sheer relief of it–is doubtless the important thing. But in the history of Romance itself–a history which stretches back to the *Odyssey* and beyond–it makes not a return but an advance or revolution: the conquest of new territory.

Nothing quite like it was ever done before. Probably no book yet written in the world is quite such a radical instance of what its author has elsewhere called 'sub-creation'. The direct debt (there are of course subtler kinds of debt) which every author must owe to the actual universe is here deliberately reduced to the minimum. Not content to create his own story, he creates, with an almost insolent prodigality, the whole world in which it is to move, with its own theology, myths, geography, history, palaeography, languages, and orders of being–a world "full of strange creatures beyond count." The names alone are a feast, whether redolent of quiet countryside (Michel Delving, South Farthing), tall and kingly (Boramit, Faramir, Elendil), loathsome like Smeagol, who is also Gollum, or frowning in the evil strength of Barad-dûr or Gorgoroth; yet best of all (Lothlorien, Gilthoniel, Galadriel) when they embody that piercing, high elvish beauty of which no other prose writer has captured so much.

David Livingstone & Books

Missionary

"I grant he is not an angel; but approaches to that being as near as the nature of a living man will allow. His gentleness never forsakes him; his hopefulness never deserts him. No harassing anxieties, distraction of mind, long separation from home and kindred, can make him complain. He thinks all will come out right at last; he has such faith in the goodness of Providence. . . .

"Another thing that specially attracted my attention was his wonderfully retentive memory. If we remember the many years he has spent in Africa, deprived of books, we may well think it an uncommon memory that can recite whole poems from Burns, Tennyson, Longfellow, Whittier, and Lowell. . . ."

The Way of Life

by Lao Tzu
Recommended by: Layne Longfellow, Ph.D.
Certified Speaking Professional

Why is it lonely at the top? Lao Tzu says: "Because a man thinks of the personal body as self. When he no longer thinks of the personal body as self, neither failure nor success can ail him. One who knows his lot to be the lot of all other men is a safe man to guide them."

Why are fatigue and stress the reward for success? Because we bend our nature toward the goals of others. Lao Tzu says, "How can a man's life keep its course if he will not let it flow? Those who flow as life flows know they need no other force. They feel no wear, they feel no tear, they need no mending, no repair."

Males, especially, are taught to know themselves through their actions, their deeds. We literally define ourselves through what we do, not what we are. We admire the cleverness of scoundrels more than the innocence of saints. Lao Tzu says, "Rather abide at the center of your being: for the more you leave it, the less you learn. Search your heart and see if he is wise who takes each turn: the way to do is to be."

But isn't this "copping out?" How do I demonstrate that I am the master of my own fate, that I am strong and not weak? Lao Tzu says, "A man with outward courage dares to die, a man with inward courage dares to live."

This book has not changed my life. My life is changing, in many ways and for many reasons. This book is a part. I allow that. When the student is ready, the teacher will appear.

Rubaiyat of Omar Khayyam

by Edward Fitzgerald
Recommended by: Anthony J. Lordi,
Insurance Executive

The book that has always captured my imagination and my time is *Rubaiyat of Omar Khayyam* by translation of Edward Fitzgerald.

"Oh come with Old Khayyam, and leave the
wise – to talk.
One thing is certain, that life flies
One thing is certain and the rest is lies.
The flower that once has blown forever dies.
As a bitter tale not to be forgotten"
"I sent my soul through the invisible,
Some letter of that after life to spell:
And after many days my soul returned –
And said "Behold myself am Heaven and hell –
How true but it is hard to face – TRUTH."

This book if read with open heart and mind – will allow us to look within ourselves and if we want to be "Honest" shows us solutions and how to help others. What a grand world we have – we should work at keeping it grand and give more than we want to get. In addition to your family – each day show love and understanding to one person. There are four billion people on this earth – that's over four billion loves a day.

WOOW!!!

Mere Christianity

by C. S. Lewis
Recommended by: Mick Luckhurst,
Football Player, Atlanta Falcons

This book is a practical application of the life I like to live, and is an excellent one to distribute to friends and people who are searching for answers.

"And that leads on to my second point. People often think of Christian morality as a kind of bargain in which God says, 'If you keep a lot of rules I'll reward you, and if you don't I'll do the other thing.' I do not think that is the best way of looking at it. I would much rather say that every time you make a choice you are turning the central part of you, the part of you that chooses, into something a little different from what it was before. And taking your life as a whole, with all your innumerable choices, all your life long you are slowly turning this central thing either into a heavenly creature or into a hellish creature; either into a creature that is in harmony with God, and with other creatures, and with itself, or else into one that is in a state of war and hatred with God, and with its fellow-creatures, and with itself. To be the one kind of creature is heaven: that is, it is joy and peace and knowledge and power. To be the other means madness, horror, idiocy, rage, impotence, and eternal loneliness. Each of us at each moment is progressing to one state or the other."

The Richest Man in Babylon

by George S. Clason
Recommended by: Frederick M. MacGee
President, The Dale Carnegie Courses

The book I have chosen is *The Richest Man in Babylon*, by George S. Clason. For anyone who wants to know about the real road to financial independence, this book is a must. It not only gives the secret to financial independence, but it gives a road map to get you there. I have read many books that promise great rewards in the area of financial planning, but as I look back over 30 years in business I must admit that financial success began for me when I put to work in my life the simple principles of this astounding book. It is amazing how things work when we keep them simple. This is a small but mighty book for anyone who really wants to gain the peace of mind that comes from being financially independent.

"'I do see good luck in a different light. I had thought of it as something most desirable that might happen to a man without effort upon his part. Now, I do realize such happenings are not the sort of thing one may attract to himself. From our discussion I have learned that to attract good luck to oneself, it is necessary to take advantage of opportunities. Therefore, in the future, I shall endeavor to make the best of such opportunities as do come to me.'"

Archibald MacLeish & Ulysses

Correspondence 3/3/75

I read Robert Fitzgerald's *Ulysses* to Ada under the hum of the reel off the south shore of Bermuda. Elinor Warren wrote me that she had listened to it when she knew she was going blind. I can see why. It lacks the marvellous "said" quality of the plays Robert and Dudley Fitts wrote together – the absolute rhythmic rightness – but it is better than any other verse translation I know and it gave me a great gift. In Book Eleven after Odysseus has taken over as the poet of his own voyage and has told the tale of the landing on the foreshore of the dead and all that followed, Alkinoos, king of the Phaiakians, reassures him:

"You speak with art, but your intent is honest.
The Argive troubles, and your own troubles,
you told as a poet would, a man who knows
the world . . . "

That last line was like the bursting of a sun. "As a poet would, a man who knows the world". Of course, I said. What else is a great poet! A man who knows the world. Who else knows the world? Who else but Shakespeare, Dante, Homer himself. So I wrote Robert. Was this truly what Homer wrote? He replied that what Homer said "might simply be taken to mean 'a man knowing in the art of song'. "Whether he did not understand or did not want to I can't make out so I have written him again. What made him use the magnificent phrase he did? If he answers I will tell you, but whether he answers or not nothing will be quite the same again for I have now the word for it – a man who knows the world."

Meditations

by Marcus Aurelius (A.D. 121–180)
Recommended by: Christine Maher, Managing Director, Celebrity Speakers, Australia

"The workings of chance are not separated from nature or without an interweaving and dependence on the dispositions of providence. From providence all things flow. And side by side with it is necessity, and that which works to the advantage of the whole universe, of which you are a part.

"As surgeons always have their instruments and knives ready for cases which suddenly need their skill, so do you have principles ready for the understanding of things divine and human, and for every act, even the smallest, remembering the bond which unites the divine and human to one another. For neither will you do any human thing well without at the same time having regard to things divine, nor vice versa.

"No longer wander at random. You shall not live to read your own memoirs . . . or the selections from books which you were reserving for your old age. Hasten then to the goal which you have before you. Throw away vain hopes and come to your own aid, while yet you may, if you care at all for yourself.

". . . let your principles be brief and fundamental, which, as soon as you shall call them to mind, will be sufficient to cleanse the soul completely, and send you back free from all discontent with the stale things to which you return."

Positive Imaging

by Dr. Norman Vincent Peale
Recommended by: Bunny Marks,
President, Crowns International

These are some thoughts I received from Dr. Peale's book *Positive Imaging*.

"There is a powerful and mysterious force in human nature that is capable of bringing about dramatic improvement in our lives. It is a kind of mental engineering that works best when supported by a strong religious faith. It's not difficult to practice; anyone can do it. Recently it has caught the attention of doctors, psychologists, and thinkers everywhere, and a new word has been coined to describe it. That word is *imaging*, derived from *imagination*.

"Imaging, the forming of mental pictures or images, is based on the principle that there is a deep tendency in human nature to ultimately become precisely like that which we imagine or image ourselves as being. An image formed and held tenaciously in the conscious mind will pass presently, by a process of mental osmosis, into the unconscious mind. And when it is accepted firmly in the unconscious, the individual will strongly tend to have it, for then it has you. So powerful is the imaging effect on thought and performance that a long-held visualization of an objective or goal can become determinative."

Peter Marshall and the Screwtape Letters

Former Chaplain, United States Senate

To most moderns, the devil is either a swear-word or an allusion to archaic folklore. Nowadays the devil has become a clown in pantomime . . . and hell a sardonic jest.

Quite in the mood of this gay, spoofing approach to the subject is the now-famous book, *The Screwtape Letters*, written by the Oxford don C. S. Lewis. The book is a series of letters from a senior devil, Screwtape, to his underling and apprentice, Wormwood.

Wormwood has been given the assignment of seeing to it that one average, middle-class Englishman never makes it to the Father's house. But underneath the blithe, sparkling facade of the book, there are deep philosophical and spiritual insights. Mr. Lewis wrote *The Screwtape Letters* not just as a humorous exercise, but for a reason.

He had important things to say: That there is a Dark Power in our world . . . That this Evil Power has intelligence and wit . . . was created by God . . . was once good . . . and went wrong. In at least forty-three separate references recorded in the Gospels, Jesus spoke of this Evil Personality, giving him a variety of names: Satan . . . the Devil . . . the Enemy . . . the Adversary, Tempter.

A loving Heavenly Father is never the author of evil, Christ insisted. He attributed to this Dark Power all disease, pain, depravity, sin and death. Hence the devil is one to be taken seriously indeed.

–Peter Marshall, *John Doe, Disciple*

Vietnam Veteran

Patton's Principles

by Porter B. Williamson
Recommended by: Clebe McClary, USMC-Retired
Author, Speaker

Patton's Principles is a handbook for managers who mean it! It should be read by everybody. We are all leaders, good or bad, up or down, in or out. I've read *Patton's Principles* four times and learned something new each time.

If our leaders had gone by his leadership in Vietnam we would have won in six months and those wonderful people would be free today.

If I had followed the principles taught in this book, I would have saved some of my men's lives and maybe saved my arm and eye.

Say what you mean and mean what you say will build winners in the office, classroom, home, athletic field or on the battlefield.

Here are a few Patton nuggets –

"Success is not how high and fast you reach the top, but how high and fast you bounce back when you hit the bottom."

"If everybody is thinking alike, somebody isn't thinking."

"The right kind of fear can have a positive effect."

Vietnam POW

The Power of Positive Thinking

by Norman Vincent Peale
Recommended by: Eugene B. McDaniel, Capt. USN
President, American Defense Foundation

I picked up *The Power of Positive Thinking* when I was a college freshman on an athletic scholarship. Dr. Peale's philosophy of faith and positive thinking helped me win ball games and, more importantly, made me decide that I could be whatever I wanted to be.

Those principles of faith and positive thinking stayed with me through a successful Navy career and helped me stay spiritually strong for six years as a prisoner of war in Vietnam. In fact, it was positive thinking and a deep faith in God that enabled me to survive my captivity and come home to freedom.

"The secret is to fill your mind with thoughts of faith, confidence, and security. This will force out or expel all thoughts of doubt, all lack of confidence. To one man who for a long time had been haunted by insecurities and fears I suggested that he read the Bible underlining in red pencil every statement it contains relative to courage and confidence. He also committed them to memory, in effect cramming his mind full of the healthiest, happiest, most powerful thoughts in the world. These dynamic thoughts changed him from cringing hopelessness to a man of compelling force. The change in him in a few weeks was remarkable. From almost complete defeat he became a confident and inspiring personality. He now radiates courage and magnetism. He regained confidence in himself and his own powers by a simple process of thought conditioning."

Vietnam POW

The Best of Sterling Sill

Recommended by: Jay R. Jensen,
Lt. Col., U.S. Air Force Retired

A book that has meant much to me is *The Best of Sterling Sill*:

"Each person must develop his own leadership. Leadership cannot be bought. It cannot be conferred. It cannot be inherited. It knows no divine right, it cannot be passed on by any process of succession. It is always stamped with the label, Not Transferable.' It is acquired only by the personal mastery of each individual aspirant. Once this ability is acquired, one may then touch the keys regulating human behavior and help to bring about the most important responses in human beings.

"Jesus tried to teach us some of these laws of leadership, most of which we have not made much of an attempt to master. For example, He gave an almost all-powerful law of success by which we may bring about in others almost any response we desire. This law is made up of just fifteen words. Some have called it the Golden Rule; others have called it the Law of the Boomerang; others have called it the Law of Retaliation. This law says, 'Whatsoever ye would that men should do unto you, do ye even so unto them.' If we could only learn to put this one law into effect, it would transform our lives and the world in thirty days."

You Can Change the World

by Father James Keller
Recommended by: Bill McGrane, CPAE, Certified Speaking Professional

The central theme of *You Can Change the World* is, "It is better to light one candle than to curse the darkness." Every life has a purpose regardless of its background or circumstances.

A great American scientist, Steinmetz, summed up the philosophy of the book in this statement from it: "I think the greatest discovery (to be made) will be along spiritual lines. Here is a force which history clearly teaches has been the greatest power in the development of man. Yet we have been merely playing with it and have never seroiusly studied it as we have social forces. Some day people will learn that material things do not bring happiness, that they are of little use in making men and women creative and forceful. Then the scientists of the world will turn their laboratories over to the study of God and prayer and the spiritual forces which as yet have been hardly scratched. When this day comes, the world will advance more in one generation than it has in the last four!"

For over 40 years I have researched the enduring principles that would stand the test of time. I have found that our level of Self-Esteem determines our interest in changing the world. Raise your Self-Esteem; then You Can Change the World.

The Prophet

by Kahlil Gibran
Recommended by: Maxine McIntyre,
Certified Speaking Professional,
The Leadership Development Institute

I would have to say that the most thought-provoking book I have read was Kahlil Gibran's *The Prophet*. From where I was in my life at the time I first read it, it changed the direction of my career.

Gibran had a way of saying things in a simply beautiful as well as saying them beautifully simple. But even more important was his attitude toward his responsibility as a writer.

After completing the manuscript in 1919, he waited four years to turn it over to his publisher, stating, "I wanted to be sure, I wanted to be very sure, that every word of it was the very best I had to offer."

Not only has his book been an inspiration to me the past fifteen years, but Gibran's philosophy has been the foundation of my life, to wit: I try to be sure that what I give as a parent, a teacher, a speaker, and a writer, is done with the very best I have to offer.

Russell Conwell and Books

Russell Conwell was always a lover of books and of the best literature. To him books were the voices of the great men and women of all ages telling him their inmost thoughts. In his early life he eagerly read and reread the few volumes which the home possessed and such as could be borrowed from neighbors. Moore was his favorite poet, with Milton a close second. He knew the works of these two by heart from constant reading, and could repeat page after page of their poetry.

Of those times he says: "It was a day of few books, and I do not know but that it is better than having so many. In my boyhood we read thoroughly what we did read. In those days, Bunyan's "Pilgrim's Progress" and the Bible were read, as it is doubtful if they are today."

Biographies were also favorite reading in those early days. The biography of Amos Lawrence and of Lord Cobden were two that greatly influenced him. Samuel Smiles' "Self Help" and Mathews' "Getting on in Life" also had a potent effect upon him.

Shakespeare was Doctor Conwell's chosen author; and his favorite characters in literature were Little Eva and Rebecca in fiction, Godfrey in poetry, Kossuth in history, Hamlet in drama, and Cicero in oratory. There are, of course, many books on theology and various doctrinal points and a scattering of general literature. But there is almost an absence of fiction. Real life – life as it has been lived by men and women who have done worth-while things – was what surrounded him when he had time to sit in his study and let his eyes rest upon the shelves that line its walls from floor to ceiling.

Thomas Merton and a Book

(1915–1968)

He saw a copy of *The Spirit of Medieval Philosophy* by Etienne Gilson in Scribner's on Fifth Avenue, he went in and bought it. Reading Gilson, he seemed to soar into a great wide landscape the existence of which he had never suspected. What seized his imagination (and it may be that this reveals him as a natural mystic) was the concept of *aseitas*. Merton wrote:

"In this one word, which can be applied to God alone, and which expresses His most characteristic attribute, I discovered an entirely new concept of God – a concept which showed me at once that the belief of Catholics was by no means the vague and rather superstitious hangover from an unscientific age that I had believed it to be. On the contrary, here was a notion of God that was at the same time deep, precise, simple and accurate and, what is more, charged with implications which I could not even begin to appreciate. *Aseitas* – simply means the power of a being to exist absolutely in virtue of itself, not as caused by itself, but as requiring no cause, no other justification for its existence except that its very nature is to exist. There can be only one such Being: That is God. And to say that God exists *a se* of and by reason of Himself, is merely to say that God is Being Itself. *Ego sum qui sum* ("I am who I am"). And this means that God must enjoy "complete independence not only as regards everything outside but also as regards everything within Himself."

This notion made such a profound impression on me that I made a pencil note at the top of the page. "Aseity of God – God is being *per se*."

– Maurice Furlong

Prescription for Tomorrow

by Harold J. Cummings
Recommended by: Paul J. Micali, President, The Lacy Institute; Certified Speaking Professional

Each chapter in this book is based on philosophies that Cummings lived by and that anyone can use. For instance, he explains how to live in peace with yourself . . . by sitting on your throne in that relatively small space just above your collar and tie. He recommends never lying awake in bed at night nursing your troubles. You should become absolute boss in your belfry and act as night watchman until sleep comes and takes over. He claims that no matter what your purpose is in life, bull-headed obstacles seem bound to arise. As long as you face them calmly, get enough sleep, sit tight on your throne, etc., you have a chance to think your way through.

Cummings makes a big point about the need to fight off three diseases. He calls them Self-Pity, Jealousy and Negative Thinking. He claims that they can "dethrone or deboss you." He insists that they are the most debilitating diseases known to humanity.

While I have been blessed with the ability to always maintain a positive outlook and to handle any setback as a challenge, I will be the first to admit that reading this little gem is something I do every so often to make sure that these divinely granted virtues stay intact.

The Knowledge of the Holy

by A. W. Tozer

Recommended by: Don Miller, Pastor

A. W. Tozer's great ministry to the church and to those of us who heard him often was to magnify the person and character of God. The God he presented from Scripture gave us deep desire to honor and magnify Him as well.

His book, *The Knowledge of the Holy*, does in print what he did so masterfully as a preacher. Here in short, pithy, glorious chapters he writes about the attributes of God. He says the number is unimportant. Faber spoke of "God of a thousand attributes" and Charles Wesley spoke of them as numberless. Tozer, in beautiful and worshipful language, writes of eighteen.

They are presented against the background of his conviction which he states early. "What comes to our mind when we think about God is the most important thing about us. The history of mankind will show that no people have ever risen above its religion and man's spiritual history will positively demonstrate that no religion has ever been greater than its idea of God. Furthermore, we tend by a secret law of the soul to move toward our mental image of God. This is true of individual Christians and also for the company of believers called the church."

If you have thought the study of the attributes of God is dull then here is the book to change your idea.

Love

by Leo Buscaglia
Recommended by: E. Larry Moles,
Certified Speaking Professional

The book, *Love*, shows you many ways in which you can be yourself and how to use what you have in the best way possible. Leo Buscaglia zeros in on ways people can find the most important areas of their life – themselves. As he says, "there has never been the same sunset twice. Look at everybody's face. Each face is different. There have never been two flowers alike."

"Live now. When you are eating – eat. When you are loving – love. When you are talking with someone – talk. When you are looking at the flowers – look. Catch the beauty of the moment."

This is life, happy now. This book, like its author, Leo Buscaglia, will help you to find yourself and life.

I've shared this book with many people in the hope that it will help them as much as it has helped me.

The Pleasures of Life

by John Lubbock
Recommended by: Alfred A. Montapert,
Executive, Author

Many years ago while browsing through Foyles Book Store in London, I came across a book titled *The Pleasures of Life*, by John Lubbock.

Immediately, I knew that I had hit gold. I hurried to the Charing Cross Hotel where I was staying and took my new found treasure to the dining room. After ordering my meal, I started devouring the book I had just purchased.

This truly was a great day for me, for I was as happy as a poor man who had just found a big bag of gold.

These words jumped off the pages . . . "Life is a great gift, and as we reach years of discretion, we must naturally ask ourselves . . . what should be the main object of our existence."

Reading such words of counsel and encouragement, I was overjoyed. Guess what? One of the chapters of *The Pleasures of Life* was "Reading Books" and another was "The Blessings of Friends." Other chapters were . . . "The Duty of Happiness," "The Value of Time," "The Pleasures of Travel," "The Pleasures of Home," "The Beauties of Nature," "The Destiny of Man," etc.

I have a big appetitie for reading, and this book is one of the best I have read. In the old days, books were rare and dear; now our difficulty is what to select. There is an art in reading. To read without reflecting is like buying coffee beans and never grinding them. The mind, like the body, is maintained not by what it swallows but by what it digests and assimilates.

The Practice of Management

by Peter F. Drucker
Recommended by: George Morrisey, CPAE, Certified Speaking Professional, Author

The one concept that has formed the foundation of my whole approach to management and personal development (and that is the underlying theme in all my books) is Drucker's concept of "Management by Objectives and Self-Control." What this "new" concept emphasized was that the most effective performance occurs when individuals clearly understand the performance goals of the business and the contribution they are expected to make. Then, they can establish their own objectives, subject to review and acceptance by their supervisors, and can monitor their own performance toward their achievement.

What a relevation! Everyone in an organization is, in fact, a manager and one of the primary responsibilities of a supervisor is to make it possible for those supervised to do an increasingly effective job of managing themselves. As "St. Peter" puts it so beautifully, "management by objectives and self-control may properly be called a philosophy of management. It rests on a concept of the job of management. It rests on an analysis of the specific needs of the management group and the obstacles it faces. It rests on a concept of human action, behavior and motivation. Finally, it applies to every manager, whatever his (or her) level and function, and to any organization whether large or small. It insures performance by converting objective needs into personal goals. And this is genuine freedom." Amen!

The Prophet

by Kahlil Gibran
Recommended by: Lily B. Moskal,
Certified Speaking Professional

My favorite book is quite small in size, yet gigantic in wisdom–*The Prophet*, by Kahlil Gibran. A good friend gave it to me while I was in college and, in return, I have given away many copies as gifts.

It is a beautiful book filled with words of wisdom on various subjects, including chapters on LOVE, on MARRIAGE, on CHILDREN, on GIVING, on JOY AND SORROW, TEACHING, and many more. It is the story of a beloved prophet, who has lived in the fantasy city of Ophalese, and his return by ship back to the isle of his birth. Before he departs, he is asked to leave behind his godly wisdom: ". . . speak to us and give us of your truth."

And he does. On love: "When love beckons to you, follow him, Though his ways are hard and steep." On Marriage: "And stand together yet not too near together: For the pillars of the temple stand apart. And the oak tree and the cypress grow not in each other's shadow."

It is simple, beautiful philosophy on living, caring and sharing; a book that all can enjoy and apply positively. My own copy is threadbare from years of reading.

Psycho-Feedback

by Paul G. Thomas
Recommended by: Bob Nelson,
Insurance Executive

Twenty-three years ago I met a person who instilled in me the necessity of feeding my mind by reading books.

Since that time I have developed a plan that allows me to read 50 books a year, or a book a week.

The book that has indeed impressed me, along with many others, is entitled *Psycho-Feedback*, by Paul G. Thomas.

Mr. Thomas starts the book with an interesting question: "Which would you say is likely to be more important to you, your willpower or your imagination?"

I answered the question – willpower – but I was wrong. The correct answer – overwhelmingly – is your imagination. He then goes on in the book to prove his point.

Mr. Thomas explains how the input and output from our personality is much like a computer. In order to have the proper habits which are extremely important, we need to buy techniques that will allow the dominant factors of our life, such as diligence, overpower the opposite of that – laziness.

He calls this system Psycho-Feedback, which is a method of controlling the human system by both reinserting into it the results of its past performance and by inserting into it the results of its present performance or experience.

This book takes time to read, but it promotes a great amount of thinking in order to understand these concepts. I most heartily recommend it.

Laws of Success

by Napoleon Hill
Recommended by: Larry Neuhoff,
Insurance Executive

I recently discovered certain principles for business and health that dramatically changed my outlook. The principles were found in the book, *Laws of Success*, authored by Napoleon Hill. The "Think and Grow Rich" author delineated the philosophies and standards of several former American heroes. The assembled laws certainly provide us with the keys to the treasure of success.

"One of the greatest problems of life, if not, in fact, the greatest, is that of learning the art of harmonious negotiation with others. This course was created for the purpose of teaching people how to negotiate their way through life with harmony and poise, free from the destructive effects of disagreement and friction which bring millions of people to misery, want and failure every year.

"With this statement of the purpose of the course you should be able to approach the lessons with the feeling that a complete transformation is about to take place in your personality.

"You cannot enjoy outstanding success in life without power, and *you can never enjoy power without sufficient personality to influence other people to cooperate with you in a spirit of harmony.*"

Motivation and Personality

by Abraham Maslow
Recommended by: Jim Newman, CPAE,
President, The Pace Organization

I was browsing through a bookstore in 1955 or '56 and found a new book with an interesting title and an even more interesting table of contents. So, I bought *Motivation and Personality* and read it. Then I read it again. I made notes in the margins, and underlined words, lines, paragraphs. Maslow's concern was with healthy behavior, not illness. What a great idea! What were the steps to becoming a "self-actualizing" person? The whole concept of a hierarchy of motivation was new, exciting and fulfilling to me. As I read that book – and other Maslow writings which followed, of course – bits and pieces of what I had been studying and exploring suddenly fit together and made sense.

Many have stood on Maslow's shoulders. A lot of exciting research, books, seminars and therapies have evolved from the doors that he opened. There is a marvelous surge of interest today in the positive aspects of human behavior. What is different about people and organizations that excel? What can a person do to become what he or she is capable of being? What can each of us do to contribute to the growth and development of other people with whom we live and work? I am sure that it has not had the same effect on everyone who has read it, but I can say with certainty that when the teacher came along, this student was ready. Thanks, Abe.

John Newton and Books

There were no persons on board to whom I could speak with freedom concerning the state of my soul, none from whom I could ask advice. As to books, I had a New Testament, Stanhope, and a volume of Bishop Beveridge's sermons, one of which, upon our Lord's passion, affected me much. In perusing the New Testament, I was struck with several passages: The fig tree (Luke 13); the case of St. Paul (1 Timothy 1); but particularly the Prodigal (Luke 15). I thought the Prodigal had never been so exemplified as by myself. The goodness of the father in receiving, nay, in running to meet such a son, as an illustration of the Lord's goodness to returning sinners, gained upon me.

Amazing Grace

by John Newton

Amazing grace! how sweet the sound,
That saved a wretch like me!
I once was lost, but now am found
Was blind, but now I see.

Ain't Nobody Better Than You

by Joe Black

Recommended by: Frederic Nicholson, Director, Corporate Development, Greyhound Corporation

This autobiography of Joe Black is a book that not only provides light reading but is inspirational, practical and one which I refer back to when things look a little dark. It still gives me a laugh and a chuckle.

Joe Black was the National League's Rookie of the Year in 1952 and became the first Black pitcher to win a World Series game. His story contains a multitude of messages that represent what I hope others would use as an attitude towards life.

"I am aware that as I moved through life that there was always someone willing to assist me, as long as I was doing things to help myself. My mother did see me accomplish some positive goals and I am thankful that she instilled her strong character within me and supported me in all my endeavors. I am glad that I was able to fill my dad's heart with pride and happiness because I was fortunate enough to be the Big League Ball player that he wished to be. My sister, Ruby, has my gratitude because she helped to make it possible for me to acquire a college education. I can never give enough praise to my sister, Phyllis. God, above, knows where she got the strength to carry on, because she took care of her family, and at the same time cared for my mother, father, and Ruby until their 'souls' were called to Heaven. . . . I praise the Lord for allowing me to project a positive image and having the ability to communicate with my nephews."

Wake Up and Live

by Dorothea Brande
Recommended by: Gene Perret,
Professional Speaker, Writer

I've always cherished a tiny book copyrighted in 1936 – Dorothea Brande's *Wake Up and Live*. It made a difference in my life for two reasons.

First, it came to me at a time when I needed it. It was a period that most of us struggle through – a time when I had to decide whether to continue to do what I "had" to do or begin something that I'd always wanted to do, but never had the courage to attempt.

This volume seemed to look me in the eye and talk directly to me. It didn't molly-coddle the reader or offer a band-aid to cover the emotional wounds. No, indeed, it said right out that if I wasn't where I wanted to be it was my fault. It wasn't because my parents made some mistakes in raising me. It wasn't because society had a vendetta against me. It wasn't because of my friends, relatives, and neighbors. It was me. The book startled me into some action because it said right to my face that I had a will to fail. Then it went on to prove it.

Secondly, *Wake Up and Live* was my introduction to self-help books. The common sense in these pages prompted me to find more of this wisdom in bookstores and libraries. I did and still do.

I'm happy that I found it and tried it, and I recommend it to you.

Self-Renewal: The Individual and the Innovative Society

by John W. Gardner
Recommended by: Bernard H. Petrina, M.A., Director, Executive-Management Renewal

John W. Gardner wrote his magnificent book, *Self-Renewal: The Individual and the Innovative Society*, in the early sixties when our society was experiencing an upheaval of change. Now, more than twenty years later, with the remarkable increase in technology that took place in those two decades, his insight and counsel is even more vital and inspiring. It is Gardner's contention that as a society or an organization ages, its hopes, dreams and energies tend to become more rigid and "buried under the weight of tradition and history." Lest we believe that all societies must eventually come to decay, Gardner suggests that the answer is Renewal, a process which allows for creativity, continuous innovation and revitalization. The subject of renewal is not the society but the individual.

The answer, as Gardner so ably expresses it, lies with each one of us. The self-renewal person appreciates the past but lives for the future. However, optimism alone will not shape the future. There is a constant need for personal responsibility that adapts creativity to change.

John W. Gardner's *Self-Renewal: The Individual and the Innovative Society* is a delightful tonic for any person who seeks direction and creative renewal in a world whose splendid mysteries have hardly been tapped.

Servant Leadership

by Robert K. Greenleaf
Recommended by: Hugh W. Pinnock,
Insurance Executive

I like *Servant Leadership* by Robert K. Greenleaf. The reasons are these:

1. We are living in a very selfish age where people concentrate upon their own needs, disregarding in an almost wholesale manner the problems and frustrations of others. *Servant Leadership* effectively teaches how we can be more sensitive in serving those who need us.

2. So many men and women appointed or called to positions of leadership fail to understand that the most effective leaders are those who are secure enough to lead from the position of a servant. *Servant Leadership* illustrates that principle many times.

3. The burden of leadership is heavy. It is time consuming, utilizing most of the energy of those in leadership positions. The book, *Servant Leadership*, removes much of the negative pressure and frustrations that come from directing others, showing individuals who occupy responsible positions that they can lead effectively from a position of kindness, courageous meekness, and openness. *Servant Leadership* restores sanity to this vital part of life.

How I Raised Myself from Failure to Success in Selling

by Frank Bettger
Recommended by: Nido Qubein, CPAE
Certified Speaking Professional, Past President, National Speakers Association, Author

As a seventeen-year-old coming to America in 1966 with no money, no knowledge of the English language, and no connections–I set out to follow the advice of my mother: "To be successful, Nido, you must first walk hand in hand and side by side with people who are already successful."

I sought to learn, through practical application, how to be a successful salesperson. That's when I first became acquainted with Frank Bettger and his outstanding book. This work taught me that leadership is basically getting people to help you pursue worthwhile goals, that people are known for what they finish and not for what they start, and that motivation without mobilization means only frustration.

A failure as a salesman at the age of twenty-nine, Frank Bettger became one of the country's outstanding producers in the next few years. In his book, he shares personal experiences in a way that I could identify with and understand. He taught me how to overcome fear of failure. He explained how to draw out a prospect, find the key issue and discover hidden objections. In short, he clearly introduced me to the secrets of effective selling.

Frank Bettger, through his book, and later through his personal example of excellence, touched my life in a personal way.

The Man from Margaree
Writings & Speeches of M. M. Coady

Edited by Alexander F. Laidlaw
Recommended by: Norman K. Rebin,
Certified Speaking Professional, Canada

Five days before Christmas '83, I gave my all-time favorite person, Delva–mistress, friend, wife-companion of 24 years–my all-time favorite book *The Man from Margaree*. As Delva lay in Ottawa's Queensway Carleton Hospital stricken with cancer, I felt possessed to pour all my affection into one simple yet supreme gesture. This book was that gesture, for it said far more eloquently than I as a seasoned speechmaker ever could, "I need you, I respect you, I love you . . . fight, hope, transcend yourself, persevere." For that is the timeless tribute that Father Moses Coady, the Man from Margaree, in the Maritimes soul of Canada, paid all the farmers, the fishermen, and the flock who attended him. Coady became a legend in his lifetime, the eternal flame that fired the fuel of self-reliance, self-sufficiency and self-help. To the oppressed, the depressed, and the repressed, in those early traumatic decades of the 20th century his message was his mission . . . be your own doctor, cure thyself. As Delva faced the surgeon's scalpel, that idea became our inspiration . . . don't give in to fate, face it, fight it, shape it. I think he was convinced that only fatalists created fatalities, that life is for those who aspire to thrive, not just survive.

With extraordinary insight and warmth, Professor Alexander Laidlaw recreates the wisdom and wit of Coady's writings and speeches in *The Man from Margaree.* He depicts a crusader, a catalyst, and a co-operator. Coady believed that self-help could best be won by co-operation rather than conflict, by adult education rather than by adult manipulation.

The Green Letters – Principles of Spiritual Growth

by Miles Stanford
Recommended by: Craig Reynolds,
All-Star Baseball Player, Houston Astros

The Principles of Spiritual Growth has had a great influence on my life. Its brief explanations of the fundamentals of Christian life have given me encouragement and hope during some of the lowest periods of my life.

"Since the work of God is essentially spiritual, it demands on spiritual people for its doing; and the measure of their spirituality will determine the measure of their value to the Lord. Because this is so, in God's mind the servant is more than the work. If we are going to come truly into the hands of God for His purpose, then we shall be dealt with by Him in such a way as to continually increase our spiritual measure. Not our interest in Christian work; our energies, enthusiasm, ambitions, or abilities; not our academic qualification, or anything that we are in ourselves, but simply our spiritual life is the basis of the beginning and growth of our service to God. Even the work, when we are in it, is used by Him to increase our spiritual measure.

"It is a mistake to measure spiritual maturity merely by the presence of gifts. By themselves they are an inadequate basis for a man's lasting influence to God. They may be present and they may be valuable, but the Spirit's object is something far greater – to form Christ in us through the working of the cross."

Positioning: The Battle for Your Mind

by Al Ries and Jack Trout
Recommended by: Karl Righter,
President, Metra Advertising, Inc.

The average American is bombarded each day with thousands of advertising messages. Radio. Television. Billboards. Newspapers. Magazines. Buses. Trucks. Taxis. Matchbooks. Mail. Skywriting. Chevrolet alone spends over $130 million annually! That's $15,000 every hour!

Obviously, advertising is a high stakes game, and the battleground is the human mind. Amazingly, most Americans know very little about the advertising strategies which play such a major role in their daily buying decisions. That's why I feel many readers will be fascinated to read this book, because it discusses one of the most successful of all advertising strategies . . . positioning.

Positioning enabled a lesser-known product such as 7-Up to experience tremendous success by "positioning" itself as the Un-Cola . . . an alternative to cola drinks. Positioning has also worked for Avis, Tylenol, Michelob, Burger King, Nyquil, and many others. The book explains how.

What is even more interesting than advertising positioning is how companies, services, countries, political candidates, and churches can also be positioned for increased awareness. But most importantly, the book tells the reader how he can position himself . . . and his career . . . for success! This requires becoming an outside-in thinker, rather than an inside-out thinker. This requires patience, courage, and strength of character!

The Three Musketeers

by Alexandre Dumas
Recommended by: Cavett Roberts, CPAE, Certified Speaking Professional, Past President National Speakers Association, Author

I once heard a great man remind us of the many reasons why we should read books.

First, there is so much more of the past than the present.

Second, unimportant events have faded into oblivion, while only the important have survived.

Third, books guarantee that the influence of great people does not pass with them, but survives for all time.

In all modesty, I would like to add a fourth blessing we derive from books. Books permit us the joy and excitement of living and experiencing in a dream world those things which we were not able to experience in our world of reality.

I learned this great lesson from the first book I ever read as a youngster, *The Three Musketeers*.

We can't live exclusively in an unreal world, born of the figments of our imagination. Yet, when we cease to hope and dream and imagine wonderful things to come, our very souls and spirits wither and die.

What boy has not used the precious quality of "imagineering" to swing through the trees with Tarzan, roam the shores of a deserted island with Robinson Crusoe, or duel for right and justice along with the Three Musketeers? Is there any normal, romantic young man who has not seen in his mind's eye Cleopatra on her knees begging for his affection, or Helen of Troy holding out her arms in supplication?

Straight Talk to Men and Their Wives

by Dr. James Dobson
Recommended by: Rev. Robert Rohm, Mesquite, Texas

In this book, Dr. Dobson explains why people leave what he calls the "straight life." The straight life is made up of daily responsibilities that are not really very exciting. They are mostly burdens that get heavy and mundane after a while.

Dr. Dobson reflects that until about thirty years ago the only socially acceptable answer to this dilemma was, "Keep plugging! You have mouths to feed, backs to clothe, a boss to please, and a home to maintain. Clench your fists and get back to work." He concludes that although the answer was not comforting, it did produce stability in families.

Today, however, four voices are calling people away from the straight life: pleasure, romanticism, extramarital sexual relations, and ego needs. Dobson explains how responding to these four voices will do two things. First, it ruins the relationship you now hold and second, ironically, it is sure to eventually lead to another straight life. "The grass is greener on the other side of the fence, but it still has to be mowed!"

The answer to the dilemma, Dobson concludes, is to bring these four voices into the existing relationship and make it one of excitement and fulfillment. Dating your spouse, keeping romantic fires alive, reserving time and energy for sexual relations, and seeking to build up each other are the keys to maintaining a happy relationship.

These thoughts and many more in the book, have confirmed in my mind that if I build these qualities into my existing relationship, it will never go bankrupt. So far the dividends have been pouring in.

Man's Search for Meaning

by Victor Frankl
Recommended by: Lester A. Rosen, CLU, Insurance Exec., Recipient of National Assn. of Life Underwriters' John Newton Russell Award

If I were to be given the choice of one book to sustain and motivate me for the rest of my life, I would select *Man's Search for Meaning*, by Victor Frankl, M.D., Ph.D. It bears witness to the incredible and unexpected extent to which a man is capable of braving and defying even the worst mental tortures while being a prisoner in the concentration camps of Auschwitz and Dachau. He completely erased thoughts of self and administered to the needs of others.

From reading this book you become aware that Frankl regards the essence of human existence to be responsibleness. He quotes the late, eminent brain surgeon, Dr. Richard Cushing, as saying, "The only way to endure life is always to have a task to complete."

Frankl was once asked the question – what would he select, what dictum or admonition to put above his desk as advice for life? He responded, "The dictum of Hillel, the ancient Jewish philosopher."

If I do not do it who else will?
If I do not do it now, when will I?
If I do it only for myself what am I?

Growing Up

by Russell Baker
Recommended by: Mark Russell,
Columnist-Comedian

Not only is this a great book but it also has the best first page of any book I've ever read.

At the age of eighty my mother had her last bad fall, and after that her mind wandered free through time. Some days she went to weddings and funerals that had taken place half a century earlier. On others she presided over family dinners cooked on Sunday afternoons for children who were now gray with age. Through all this she lay in bed but moved across time, traveling among the dead decades with a speed and ease beyond the gift of physical science.

"Where's Russell?" she asked one day when I came to visit at the nursing home.

"I'm Russell," I said.

She gazed at this improbably overgrown figure out of an inconceivable future and promptly dismissed it.

"Russell's only this big," she said, holding her hand, palm down, two feet from the floor. That day she was a young country wife with chickens in the backyard and a view of hazy blue Virginia mountains behind the apple orchard, and I was a stranger old enough to be her father.

Early one morning she phoned me in New York. "Are you coming to my funeral today?" she asked.

Carl Sandburg and Books

The first biography I owned was of a size I could put in one of my vest pockets. I was going along to the Seventh Ward school when I found it on a sidewalk. The front cover had gloss paper and a color picture of the head and shoulders of a two-star general in a Confederate gray uniform. The title read *A Short History of General P. T. Beauregard*. There were thirteen pages of reading in fine print. Inside the back cover was a list of a "Series of Small Books," histories of Civil War generals, fifty of them, with a notice of "other series in preparation." And here you learned how to get these books. It said "Packed in Duke's Cigarettes." I couldn't think of buying ten-cent packages of Duke's Cameo or Duke's Cross-Cut cigarettes for the sake of filling my vest pockets with histories, nice as they were.

I scouted around and found three men who smoked Duke's Cigarettes "once in a while for a change." One of them was saving the books for himself. The other two saved them for me. After a while I had the histories of Beauregard, Cornelius Vanderbilt, and Sarah Bernhardt, *The Life of T. De Witt Talmage*, and the lives of George Peabody, James B. Eads, Horace B. Claflin, and Robert Ingersoll. They changed from History of to Life of.

There were days I carried the eight books, four in the upper right-hand vest pocket and four in the upper left. I had books I didn't have to take back to the Seventh Ward school or the Public Library. I was a book-owner.

Lee

by Douglas S. Freeman
Recommended by: Willard Scott
N.B.C. Today Show

To my way of thinking, Lee embodied the qualities of refinement and nobility that represented the best of the Old South. He lived by an almost chivalrous code of honor, according to which a man's word was his only contract. All of his life Lee conducted himself in such a way as to bring honor upon himself and the people he loved around him.

At the beginning of the War Between the States, Lee was offered the command of the Union Army by Lincoln. He refused the command and resigned his commission in the United States Army where he had an outstanding record. He stayed with the South, because his first duty was to his family, and he considered the whole state of Virginia his family.

He didn't come from a wealthy family. His father was a bad businessman who had lost almost everything. After his father died, Lee lived with his mother in Alexandria. He went to West Point, fought in the Mexican War, and served in the Corp of Engineers. One of his jobs was chief engineer on a project to build the levees along the Mississippi that are still there holding back the flood waters.

He married the Custis girl who was Martha Washington's great-granddaughter. His family had slaves over in Arlington, but Lee himself never owned a slave in his life.

After the war, his sense of duty led him to pledge allegiance to the Union and devote his life to service. He became president of a poor, faltering institution that later became Washington and Lee. There he worked to train a generation of Southerners in the noble ideals he cherished.

It Takes a Long Time to Become Young

by Garson Kanin
Recommended by: Arthur Secord, CPAE, Author

This book is a declaration of war on enforced retirement.

Each day of the year, four thousand Americans reach the age of 65. On that day they enter what is called "statutory senility." They are declared, legally, to be superannuated, obsolete, useless.

The book labels the Social Security Act as one of the best intentioned yet ill-advised acts ever undertaken by the United States Government.

Before this act, the Federal Government had no provision for retirement at any age, nor did most businesses.

Why 65? Professor Douglas Brown of Princeton, who was on the committee that drew up the bill, says, "I can remember no suggestion of another age." The retirement age of 65 was set in 1881 by Chancellor Otto von Bismarck when he established the first known social security program. His actuaries assured him that few Germans lived beyond that age. It would, therefore, look effective and be relatively inexpensive.

At that time the life span was 40. Today it is 70. One hundred years from now it will predictably be 90. People are living longer but being forced to retire younger. If a human being is made to retire at 50 and then lives productively to 90, some thought must be given to that forty-year span.

The book documents outstanding contributions that have been made by "old" people through the ages. It should be required reading for everyone old enough to work.

How to Win Friends and Influence People

by Dale Carnegie
Recommended by: Steven R. Shallenberger, President & CEO, Eagle Systems International

It is my belief that there are common traits or principles that cause outstanding success. Dale Carnegie brings those principles and traits together in one place in *How to Win Friends & Influence People.*

Although credit for the success I have experienced goes to those wonderful individuals who have taken the time to help me, *How to Win Friends & Influence People* has also influenced me immeasurably. Every day, I use the skills and principles taught in that book. Highlights of a few of the fine principles shared in that classic are as follows:

Understanding, Compassion, Forgiveness.

"Any fool can criticize, condemn, and complain – and most fools do.

"But it takes character and self-control to be understanding and forgiving.

"'A great man shows his greatness,' said Carlyle, 'by the way he treats little men.'

"As Dr. Johnson said: 'God Himself, sir, does not propose to judge man until the end of his days.'

"Why should you and I?"

Obviously, being an expert in certain skills leads to success; but good success can be made great success by constant familiarization with the principles eloquently taught by Dale Carnegie in the book, *How to Win Friends & Influence People.*

Getting Through to People

by Jesse S. Nirenberg
Recommended by: Robert R. Sharp, President, Peninsula Motor Club

I have just finished rereading *Getting Through to People*. This book discusses the techniques of persuasion – how to break through the mental and emotional barriers that continually obstruct the flow of ideas from one person to another. It describes the importance of clear communication, as opposed to just exchanging words, and how to keep individuals focused on your message. When feeding ideas to anyone, you should only give them one at a time. In an effort to save time, executives too often crowd the message.

Becoming a good listener is like putting together a jig-saw puzzle. Hearing the words is like receiving the pieces. However, listening meaningfully is putting the sentences together to form a complete picture. Corporate executives must be able to deal with people's emotions and thoughts. They have to deal with resistance and be able to measure the value of an idea. I found this book encourages those who read it to develop these skills and more, thus making the individual a stronger and better communicator.

Fulton Sheen & Books

Since my life has covered such a long span, it has undergone several influences in style. The greatest influence in writing was G. K. Chesterton, who never used a useless word, who saw the value of a paradox and avoided what was trite. At a later date came the writings of C. S. Lewis, who, with Chesterton and Belloc, became one of the leading apologists of Christianity in the contemporary world. Lewis' style was concrete, pedestrian, full of examples, analogies, parables and always interesting. Malcolm Muggeridge, too, has become another inspiration to me. He is always sparkling, brilliant, explosive, humorous. And I must not forget poetry, particularly *The Oxford Book of Mystical Verse*–especially the poems of Studdert Kennedy and above all Francis Thompson. Through the years I have kept a file of favorite poems many of which I have learned by heart.

Lincoln, the War Years

by Carl Sandburg

and

Lincoln, a Novel

by Gore Vidal

Recommended by: John Shumaker,
Pennsylvania State Senator

In both Sandburg's non-fiction *Lincoln, the War Years*, and Gore Vidal's fictional, *Lincoln, a Novel*, I was and am still impressed by the commentary on the last minute addition of the words "under God" by Lincoln to his Gettysburg Address. The referenced statement is "that these dead shall not have died in vain, that the nation shall *under God* have a new birth of freedom and that government of the people, by the people and for the people shall not perish from the earth."

Sandburg's *Lincoln* states, ". . . in the copy held in his hands while facing the audience he had not written the words 'under God,' though he did speak those words and included them in later copies which he wrote."

In Gore Vidal's *Lincoln,* it states, ". . . that these dead shall not have died in vain; that the nation shall, he paused a moment then said 'under God' . . . Seward nodded – his advice has been taken. Nico whispered to Hay, 'He just added that. It's not in the text.'"

This historical incident has been overlooked by many but its impact cannot be ignored. At the very last moment, or at some time after preparing his last draft the evening before, Lincoln realized what had brought this country to greatness and what was necessary to heal and rebind the wounds of a great Civil War – "one nation under God." It was fitting then and is fitting now.

How to Win Friends and Influence People

by Dale Carnegie
Recommended by: Jerry Simmons, CPAE, Certified Speaking Professional, President, The Idea Management Company

The book that I would choose that had the most profound effect on my life is *How to Win Friends & Influence People*, by Dale Carnegie. I first read it in high school, enjoyed it and began practicing its principles. I have virtually memorized this document and can attest to the fact that following its principles will enich a person's life and move them a long way toward reaching their full potential:

"There is one all-important law of human conduct. If we obey that law, we shall almost never get into trouble. In fact, that law, if obeyed, will bring us countless friends and constant happiness. But the very instant we break the law, we shall get into endless trouble. The law is this: Always make the other person feel important. John Dewey, as we have already noted, said that the desire to be important is the deepest urge in human nature; and William James said: "The deepest principle in human nature is the craving to be appreciated.' As I have already pointed out, it is this urge that differentiates us from the animals. It is this urge that has been responsible for civilization itself.

"So let's obey the Golden Rule, and give unto others what we would have others give unto us.

"How? When? Where? The answer is: All the time, everywhere."

Black Book of Polish Jewry. An Account of the Martyrdom of Polish Jewry Under Nazi Occupation

edited by Jacob Apenszlak, 1943
Recommended by: Merrill Simon, Author, Lecturer

"The testimony given by Jewish refugees . . . all reveals the same pattern in the German conduct towards the Jewish population from the start of the invasion. . . . The device consisted of isolating the Jews from the rest of the population by segregation, of 'softening' them by breaking down their moral resistance, weakening them physically by terror, hard labor, undernourishment, unhygienic conditions, lack of medical attention and by expropriating their wealth.

"But these were merely the preliminaries. After the Jews had been duly humiliated, shocked, terrorized and exhausted there followed the introduction of laws and decrees designed to prepare the defenseless and morally and physically worn out victims for their final destruction by mass slaughter.

". . . of the 1,900,000 Polish Jews who cannot be accounted for, the majority in all probability perished in the process of deportation, and, especially since the middle of 1942, by mass-extermination, and the remainder, except for those who are refugees in Russia, deported for forced labor in the East and doomed to perish, unless a quick victory for the United Nations brings them liberation, together with the liberation of all the world. No tragedy in the history of the world can be compared in its extent and in its results with this indescribable tragedy of Polish Jewry."

Aleksandr Solzhenitsyn on Tvardovsky and Tyorkin

Long ago, at the front, I had taken note of *Vasily Tyorkin* as a remarkable feat: long before the appearance of the first truthful books about the war (since Nekrasov's *In the Trenches of Stalingrad*, not so many of them have succeeded – perhaps half a dozen in all), amid the fume and crackle of gibbering propaganda which always accompanied our bombardments. Tvardovsky had succeeded in writing something timeless, courageous and unsullied, helped by a rare sense of proportion, all his own, or perhaps by a sensitive tact not uncommon among peasants. (This sensitivity beneath the coarsened and uncouth peasant exterior, and in spite of the hardships of peasant life, never ceases to astonish me.) Though he was not free to tell the whole truth about the war, Tvardovsky nevertheless always stopped just one millimeter short of falsehood, and nowhere did he ever overstep the one-millimeter mark. The result was a miracle. I am not speaking only for myself; I had excellent opportunities to observe its effects on soldiers in my battery during the war. It was the peculiarity of our job as a sound-ranging unit that they had a great deal of time, even in combat conditions, to listen to readings (at night, at field signal posts, while someone would read from the communications center). Of the many things offered them, they obviously had a special preference for *War and Peace* and *Vasily Tyorkin*.

Atlas Shrugged

by Ayn Rand
Recommended by: Philip D. Steffen, Certified Speaking Professional

When I read this book, I had been a citizen of the greatest nation on earth for twenty-eight years. However, I really didn't know what a fantastic privilege that was until the late Ms. Rand guided me and removed the blinders. Like so many Americans, I had taken for granted the bounties we enjoy in this country. And, like many others, I seldom thought about losing these gifts, assuming things would always be this way. What I failed to see was HOW we achieved all of these wonderful things.

It soon became crystal clear to me that PEOPLE, individuals like you and I, are the greatest resource we have in this land of abundance. People achieve, people create and each man and woman has the capacity to reach out, strive and seek the self satisfaction and financial rewards of their accomplishments. There are no "great people," just ordinary people who set their sights high and refuse to quit, even in the face of seemingly insurmountable obstacles. America offers the opportunity but Ms. Rand made it clear that there are those who "want" but will make no effort to "get." They live their lives expecting others to provide for them, thinking that their country and government OWE them a living. She paints a vivid, startling picture of how easy we can lose our bounty when the purveyors of socialism spread their cancer.

Atlas Shrugged opened my eyes and gave me the courage to strive for excellence. It is the BIBLE OF FREE ENTERPRISE.

Your Most Enchanted Listener

by Wendell Johnson
Recommended by: Lyman Steil,
President, Communication Development Inc.

Your Most Enchanted Listener is a book of timeless importance that deals in a constructive fashion with the problems we have in trying to live with ourselves and others. Utilizing the universal concepts of general semantics, the late Wendell Johnson provides direction that will help every individual committed to maximizing their, and others, productive behavior. And it is no secret that a pressing need exists in today's world to maximize our productive relationships through enhanced communication.

Find, read, and apply the concepts of *Your Most Enchanted Listener* to the people you meet, and the world will be a better place:

"There is a trickery about our senses that makes our seeing all suspect."

"We are remarkably adept at believing what we have never seen – at seeing what we have come to believe."

"There was an old codger who said, 'Believe in baptism? Of course. I've seen it done.'"

"To be human is to speak. To be abundantly human is to speak freely and fully."

"The realization toward which we are beckoned by these reflections is that if we are to become as fully human as we might we must not only talk freely . . . but we must wholly listen too."

"The wise man knows what the questions are."

Reflections on a Philosophy

by Dr. Forrest Shaklee
Recommended by: Dave Stoltzfus,
President, Onesimus Enterprises, Inc.

This book deals with man's thought processes. Shaklee says, "your future life will be exactly what you decide to make it, because every thought that has ever been produced by man or ever will be produced is already here on this earth now. We are blanketed by the vibrations of these thoughts. We need only to recognize them, to hear them, to learn to understand them. It is not a question of developing the power within. You have, no doubt, many times the amount of power needed or used. It is only a matter of developing your ability to use it. What demands are you making upon the power? Are you asking for pennies, or possibly nickels and dimes, when you should be asking for dollars? Do you consider this a show of humble reverence by asking for the crumbs of happiness that fall from the table of others when you should be asking for a full-course dinner? You must get in there and fight for what you want. It's yours for the thinking. It will not be handed to you on a silver platter. You must earn your way and by earning your way, I mean that you must think your way through life. Thoughts produce action and only through action can you attain that which is worthwhile."

It's a book that is only 71 pages long, but each paragraph is filled with thought-provoking ideas.

Actualizations: You Don't Have to Rehearse to Be Yourself

by Stewart Emery
Recommended by: Karen Studebaker, Director, Studebaker Psychology Centre, Singapore

Living in South East Asia for ten years and working as a therapist in an achievement-oriented society, one begins to develop an intensity and seriousness of purpose that is devoid of humor. If there is anything missing in this tropical paradise, it is laughter resulting from personal interaction.

One can occasionally catch a TV program interjected with humor or hear the unexpected insertion of one-liners from a good public speaker; but in everyday life the use of humor in communication is minimal or, more frequently, entirely absent.

How nice to come across a book on personal development in which humor is an integral part. Stewart Emery's *Actualizations: You Don't Have to Rehearse to Be Yourself* is such a book.

As a psychologist in private practice, with limited access to opportunities for upgrading skills, immersion in books is almost total. As I read *Actualizations*, I suddenly find myself reading a book with contents which will serve not only as a useful tool, but which keep me laughing. Gradually the therapist in me retreats and I emerge, absorbing, devouring, and embracing the contents of this book for the essence of myself. My professional facade slips away and the inner self wants more Emeryisms. It is magnetic. I begin to scan it for a favorite passage and find that scanning turns into hours of re-reading, marking sections useful to my present needs, and getting something new from a statement not noticed in the past. *Actualizations* is addictive.

Evangelists

Billy Sunday, the Student 1862–1935

"I never heard Billy Sunday use an ungrammatical sentence," remarked one observer. "He uses a great deal of slang, and many colloquialisms, but not a single error in grammar could I detect. Some of his passages are really beautiful English."

Sunday has made diligent effort to supplement his lack of education. He received the equivalent of a high-school training in boyhood, which is far more than Lincoln ever had. Nevertheless he has not had the training of the average educated man, much less of a normal minister of the gospel. He is conscious of his limitations: and has diligently endeavored to make up for them. When coaching the Northwestern University baseball team in the winter of '87 and '88, he attended classes at the university. He has read a great deal and to this day continues his studies. Of course his acquaintance with literature is superficial; but his use of it shows how earnestly he has read up on history and literature and the sciences. He makes better use of his knowledge of the physical sciences, and of historical allusions, than most men drilled in them for years. He displays a proneness for what he himself would call "high-brow stuff," and his disproportionate display of his "book learning" reveals his conscious effort to supply what does not come to him naturally.

Evangelists

Billy Graham & Books

"Billy Graham once took me to his study in his former home in Montreat, North Carolina. It was a comfortable, pine-paneled, second-floor room, supplied with a work desk, typewriter, dictaphone, and tape recorder. Several shelves were stacked with his sermons – he has several hundred in outline – in black looseleaf notebooks. The room was well stocked with books, none of them recent fiction; few nonreligious, save a second-hand edition of Shakespeare, several other standard classics, and a number of biographies. There were scores of books of devotional bent and religious experience and of sermons by preachers ancient and modern – the modern ones being chiefly sermons of evangelists. Nearest at hand were a Concordance and the Bible in several translations.

"He was spending, then, four to five hours a day in his study. But studying is a practice he pursues, I think, less from pleasure than from apprehension. He told me that, several years before, he had come upon a statement by the late Senator William Edgar Borah that William Jennings Bryan would have been President of the United States 'if he had read more and spoken less.'

"'That hit me with a tremendous jolt,' he said. 'I suddenly realized I was speaking more and reading less. Maybe I was starting to coast a bit mentally. Since then I've spent more time in this study and got in more hours of reading on my trips.'"

– Stanley High

Tyranny of the Urgent

by Charles E. Hummel
Recommended by: Charles Swindoll,
Pastor, Fullerton, CA

"*The Tyranny of the Urgent* is a small booklet with a big fist. Its message is uncomplicated and direct. Actually, it's a warning to all of us. There are times when its penetrating blow punches my light out! Like a guided missile, it assaults and destroys all excuses I may use.

"Here, in one sentence, is the warning: Don't let the urgent take the place of the important in your life. Oh, the urgent will really fight, claw, and scream for attention. It will plead for our time and even make us think we've done the right thing by calming its nerves. But the tragedy of it all is this: When you and I were putting out the fires of the urgent (an everyday affair), the important was again left in a holding pattern. And interestingly, the important is neither noisy nor demanding. Unlike the urgent, it patiently and quietly waits for us to realize its significance.

"Forgetting the urgent for a few minutes, ask yourself what is really important to you. What do you consider 'top priority' in your life? That is a big question, maybe one you need some time to think about."

Caught in the Conflict

by Leilani Watt
Recommended by: Donald A. Thoren,
President, The Thoren Group

When you meet a college sophomore who is the future bride of your best friend, you don't expect to have your life perspective altered by a book she would write 27 years later. But that is what happened to me.

Most of Leilani Watt's life was spent avoiding conflict. When her husband James became Secretary of the Interior she was ill-equipped for the turmoil that national news coverage would bring to their lives.

She provides insight into the pressures of the Cabinet members and their families. I learned from her revelation that conflict only brings out what is already in us. As a consultant and professional speaker, I had pretended objectivity, was uncomfortable with conflict, and either sought consensus or dealt with conflict through avoidance. She helped me realize I was ill-equipped for it, too; and what she learned, I could also learn.

All organizations today, from the family to General Motors, are changing rapidly. A key to success is building the interpersonal skills to cope competently with the inevitable conflicts. Leilani's practical and spiritual solutions have given me confidence. I can cope with greater conflict in the pursuit of my beliefs.

Think and Grow Rich

by Napoleon Hill
Recommended by: John Todd, CLU, Insurance Exec., Recipient of the National Assn. of Life Underwriters' John Newton Russell Award

The book that introduced me to the concept of the "Law of Mind" was *Think and Grow Rich*, by Napoleon Hill. My only criticism of the book has always been its title, which implies money–but the riches that come to one through application of the law of mind far transcend only the material.

"Here is an idea that has helped me enormously over the years. It is based upon the belief that there is a law of mind that is just as inexorable and just as sure as the law of gravity. You probably know this law and have used it either consciously or subconsciously to attain your present level of success, but let me try to state it as simply as I can.

"That law says that anything which you:

1. Ardently desire
2. Vividly imagine
3. Honestly believe in and
4. Expectantly act toward

will inevitably come to pass."

How to Develop Self Confidence and Influence People by Public Speaking

by Dale Carnegie
Recommended by: Phil Tornabene, Commonwealth Business Systems—USA—Australia

Personal growth always means increased production, but increased production does not always mean personal growth.

Through being deeply involved in direct sales all of my working life, I was exposed to the benefits of reading good books. Like everyone else, I guess I was looking for the "right" formula which would help me sell more. It was through this activity that I found the opening statement to be true.

It's funny how things happen in your life. I read Dale Carnegie's book *How to Develop Self Confidence and Influence People by Public Speaking*, when I was 19, and I didn't realize how much it helped me until maybe 20 years later.

The whole area of public speaking was of tremendous assistance in many situations other than speaking in public. For example: Because of the poise and self-confidence one gains, it was immediately useful to me for the following: (1) Job interviews; (2) Sales situations; (3) Negotiating a contract; and, at times, (4) Talking to a policeman about a speeding ticket.

Everything we do, whether business or personal, involves relating to others. We never get a second chance to make a good first impression. So, for me, the art outlined in this book is of paramount importance.

Man's Search for Meaning

by Viktor Frankl
Recommended by: George B. Trotta,
Sr. VP, Metropolitan Insurance Company

The theme of this book is that "man can endure an incredible amount of suffering . . . so long as he has a purpose for which to suffer. . . . " This particular message has given me strength at times and has also helped me in assisting others during their time of trial.

"A thought transfixed me: for the first time in my life I saw the truth as it is set into song by so many poets, proclaimed as the final wisdom by so many thinkers. The truth – that love is the ultimate and the highest goal to which man can aspire. Then I grasped the meaning of the greatest secret that human poetry and human thought and belief have to impart. *The salvation of man is through love and in love*. I understood how a man who has nothing left in this world still may know bliss, be it only for a brief moment, in the contemplation of his beloved. In a position of utter desolation, when man cannot express himself in positive action, when his only achievement may consist in enduring his sufferings in the right way – an honorable way – in such a position man can, through loving contemplation of the image he carries of his beloved, achieve fulfillment. For the first time in my life I was able to understand the meaning of the words, "The angels are lost in perpetual contemplation of an infinite glory.'"

Barbara Tuchman and The Scottish Chiefs

History began to exert its fascination upon me when I was about six, through the medium of the Twins series by Lucy Fitch Perkins. I became absorbed in the fortunes of the Dutch Twins; the Twins of the American Revolution, who daringly painted the name *Modeerf*, or "freedom" spelled backward, on their row boat; and especially the Belgian Twins, who suffered under the German occupation of Brussels in 1914.

After the Twins, I went through a G. A. Henry period and bled with Wolfe in Canada. Then came a prolonged Dumas period, during which I became so intimate with the Valois kings, queens, royal mistresses, and various Ducs de Guise that when we visited French *chateaux* I was able to point out to my family just who had stabbed whom in which room. Conan Doyle's *The White Company* and, above all, Jane Porter's *The Scottish Chiefs* were the definitive influence. As the noble Wallace, in tartan and velvet tam, I went to my first masquerade party, stalking in silent tragedy among the twelve-year-old Florence Nightingales and Juliets. In the book the treachery of the Countess of Mar, who betrayed Wallace, carried a footnote that left its mark on me. "The crimes of this wicked woman," it said darkly, "are verified by history."

Man's Search for Meaning

by Viktor Frankl
Recommended by: Jim Tunney, CPAE, NFL Referee, President, The Institute for the Study of Motivation and Achievement

Viktor Frankl's *Man's Search for Meaning* taught me that, of all the freedoms I have and all of the freedoms that can be taken away from me, the one freedom no one can ever take away is the freedom to choose my attitude with which I approach any problem, task, or opportunity.

"In this book, Dr. Frankl explains the experience which led to his discovery of logotherapy. As a long-time prisoner in bestial concentration camps he found himself stripped to naked existence. His father, mother, brother, and his wife died in camps or were sent to the gas ovens, so that, excepting for his sister, his entire family perished in these camps. How could he – every possession lost, every value destroyed, suffering from hunger, cold and brutality, hourly expecting extermination – how could he find life worth preserving? A psychiatrist who personally has faced such extremity is a psychiatrist worth listening to. He, if anyone, should be able to view our human condition wisely and with compassion. Dr. Frankl's words have a profoundly honest ring, for they rest on experiences too deep for deception. What he has to say gains in prestige because of his present position on the Medical Faculty of the University of Vienna and because of the renown of the logotherapy clinics that today are springing up in many lands, patterned on his own famous Neurological Policlinic in Vienna."

– Gordon W. Allport

Authentic Christianity

by Ray C. Stedman
Recommended by: Jack A. Turpin,
Chairman, Hall Mark Electronics Corp.

A book that has influenced my life's direction is *Authentic Christianity*, by Ray C. Stedman, pastor of Peninsula Bible Church in Palo Alto, California.

Many life influencing concepts are thoroughly presented by Stedman, all coming from his exposition of segments of II Corinthians. Among these concepts I will list three as they were meaningful to me.

First, "our sufficiency is from God. Nothing coming from us; everything coming from God! That is the secret of human sufficiency. It is His (Jesus) life in us that is the power by which we live a true Christian life." This concept dramatically applies to an ambitious, entrepreneural type businessman such as me.

Second, as believers mature, "we are being changed into His likeness from one degree of glory to another." This is what we often call "Christian growth" or "growing in grace." This concept was comforting – to realize our growth is gradual and that we cannot achieve it on our own schedule.

Third, "the real problem of Christian life is not how to discover the will of God. The real problem is to want to do it. It is the issue of motivation." Paul's letter outlines the believer's two primary motivations – the fear of God and the love of Jesus Christ that flows from Christ through us to others.

Mark Twain, the Learner

1601 was the letter which I wrote to Twichell, about 1876, from my study at Quarry Farm one summer day when I ought to have been better employed. I remember the incident very well. I had been diligently reading up for a story which I was minded to write, *The Prince and the Pauper*. I was reading ancient English books with the purpose of saturating myself with archaic English to a degree which would enable me to do plausible imitations of it in a fairly easy and unlabored way. In one of these old books I came across a brief conversation which powerfully impressed me, as I had never been impressed before, with the frank indelicacies of speech permissible among ladies and gentlemen in that ancient time. I was thus powerfully impressed because this conversation seemed real, whereas that kind of talk had not seemed real to me before. It had merely seemed Rabelaisian – exaggerated, artificial, made up by the author for his passing needs. It had not seemed to me that the blushful passages in Shakespeare were of a sort which Shakespeare had actually heard people use but were inventions of his own, liberties which he had taken with the facts under the protection of a poet's license.

But here at last was one of those dreadful conversations which commended itself to me as being absolutely real, and as being the kind of talk which ladies and gentlemen did actually indulge in in those pleasant and lamented ancient days now gone from us forever. I was immediately full of a desire to practice my archaics and contrive one of those stirring conversations out of my own head.

Modern Times

by Paul Johnson
Recommended by: E. A. Vastyan, Chairman College of Medicine, The Milton S. Hershey Medical Center, Pennsylvania State University

Encouraging people to read is laudatory. What an a-historical generation we're rearing these days: youngsters with no idea of the struggle and sacrifice that have been expended to provide them the inanities of television! What title would I recommend? Paul Johnson's *Modern Times*, a superb history by the editor of Britan's *Economist*, a long-overdue corrective to the pervasive influence of Karl Marx on the historiography of our time:

"What is important in history is not only the events that occur but the events that obstinately do not occur. The outstanding non-event of modern times was the failure of religious belief to disappear. . . .

"The holistic principle of moral corruption operates a satanic Gresham's Law, in which evil drives out good . . . when the moral restraints of religion and tradition, hierarchy and precedent, are removed, the power to suspend or unleash catastrophic events does not devolve on the impersonal benevolence of the masses but falls into the hands of men who are isolated by the very totality of their evil natures."

Reality Therapy

by William Glasser
Recommended by: Paul Velencia
Insurance Executive, Harrisburg, PA

Dr. Glasser helped me to appreciate my mother for what she was, one of the world's great amateur psychiatrists.

Reality Therapy might best be summarized by Glasser's emphasis on the 3 radical R's – reality, responsibility, right and wrong. The basic tenets he set forth in his book are revolutionary when contrasted with conventional therapy and Freud's understanding of behavior. Most of us completely deny the reality of the world around us and create our own more comfortable surroundings. In the real world, the beginning of reality demands us to be involved with people. Secondly, Glasser defines responsibility as the "ability to fulfill one's needs." He goes on to define right or moral behavior like this, "When a man acts in such a way that he gives and receives love and feels worthwhile to himself and others, his behavior is right or moral."

The few fundamental truths that Glasser develops – all people must be meaningfully involved with other people; teaching responsibility is done by exhibiting responsible behavior, whatever the cost; and are indeed acceptable moral standards that promote a sense of right and wrong – simply reinforce what my mother told me a thousand times over. The best things in life (love, trust, belonging) are always free and the best stuff of life (truth, understanding, wisdom) is never new. For everyone who still hasn't realized how accomplished Mama was as a human relations expert, please read Bill Glasser's book and smile – your mother will understand.

Wernher Von Braun & Books

by Erik Bergaust

The von Braun family lifestyle in Alabama was dedicated to a wholesome home life. In fact, a visitor would almost sense a dim coziness in the von Braun home, where constructive conversation, reading and music were the most important ingredients. The von Brauns rarely left their home at night. Although the style of their home life was unpretentious, a visitor would notice an Old-World flair and a serene esteem for beautiful things, from flower vases to plates and candlesticks. Most of all, perhaps, a visitor would notice that the family took great pride in owning an impressive number of books, including some very substantial volumes of serious works. A lot of reading was always done in the von Braun home. Personally, he always enjoyed travel adventures, such as the stories of the conquests of the Himalayas or Thor Heyerdahl's ocean crossings, and he continues to read a good deal of history and politics. In fact, von Braun has always complained about not having enough time to read, and if one asks him what he intends to do when he – or if he – is ready to retire some day, he will invariable answer that he wants to read – and read. "There's so much to be read," he says, "I'm sometimes stunned at the thought of how much reading I have to and want to do."

Maria Von Trapp & Books

The real highlights of these years were the meetings with my father. But they were not normal meetings of a five- or six- or seven-year-old with an elderly father who might take her on his lap and tell her stories. No, it was altogether different. My father could not adjust any longer to the life of an engineer. Something was broken in him. He could not continue a plain ordinary life like any of his collegueas. When he returned from those many years of absence, I was told he came back knowing how to speak and write in fourteen languages. He returned with cases and cases of books and instruments. Taking a large apartment in a very good section of Vienna, he filled the rooms with his books so that you couldn't see the original color of the wallpaper anywhere. When I was walking around looking at strange titles of his books, he might pick out one, maybe in Arabic.

I can't help but feel sorry that my father didn't live until my teen year, because then he would have been delighted: I was an avid reader.

But when I was nine years old, my father was found dead in his easy chair. He had slipped away during a nap.

That was the end of my childhood.

Iacocca, an Autobiography

by Lee Iacocca with William Novak
Recommended by: Leland Waggoner, CLU,
President, Virginia Life Insurance Co. of N.Y.

I think the autobiography of Lee Iacocca is an exciting and inspirational book that is of interest and value to a great many people. My feeling is that the book encompasses not just the thought of a brilliant executive and, most importantly can be an inspiration for people in every profession – especially when they have adversities in their business life. Lee Iacocca's overcoming them indeed makes an interesting story.

"Our parents came here and were part of the industrial revolution that changed the face of the world. Now there's a new high-tech revolution and everyone's scared out of their wits. When you're in a mode of change, as we're in right now, the great fear is that a lot of people are going to get hurt – and that one of those people might just turn out to be you. That's why so many people are worried. They're asking themselves: 'Will we be as good as our parents in coping with these new changes, or will we be left out in the cold?' And our kids are beginning to ask: Do we have to lower our expectations and our standard of living?

"Well, I want to say to them: It doesn't have to be that way. If our grandparents could overcome, maybe you can, too. You may never have thought about it, but they went through hell. They gave up a lot. They wanted your life to be better than theirs.

"When the chips were down, my mother found nothing wrong with working in the silk mills so I could have lunch money for school. She did what she had to do. When I got to Chrysler I found a royal mess, but I did what I had to do."

Autobiography of Ben Franklin

Recommended by: Dottie Walters,
Certified Speaking Professional, Author

I love Ben's spirit of organization: the library in Philadelphia; the post office; his Junta Society of Friends who met to do each other good; the fire association; the militia; the invention of water fins to swim with; the charting of the great rivers of the sea; the forgiving of his enemy who tried to stop the delivery of the *Saturday Evening Post*. (His rival happened to be Postmaster General under the King. When Ben became Postmaster under the new regime, his first move was to invite his rival to use the mails to deliver his publication.) Each event in Ben's life is a lesson in good business.

Franklin was a master strategist, inventor, statesman, patriot, poet, author, motivator . . . and so much more.

He was a mighty genius who tells us in simple words the way to think clearly. He tickles our funny bone and makes us laugh. He loved his children. It did not matter that the mother of his son was not married to Ben. Ben loved the child and raised him, as he did his grandson. He loved men. Loved women. Loved freedom. Gave all his inventions to the world. Ben constantly advises me to think things out! Find the good and abundant solutions. To overcome my problems by going around them, then to thank God for their fewness. To keep my eyes ever open for the opportunities flooding around us. To inspire others to do good by doing all the good that I can myself every day.

Go and find Ben! His *Autobiography* is a treasure.

Lee, the Last Years

by Charles Bracelen Flood
Recommended by: J. Michael Waters
Arthur Young & Co.

In reading *Lee, the Last Years*, I came to appreciate Robert E. Lee in an entirely different light. When many of his contemporaries lived out the rest of their lives in defeated bitterness, Lee repeatedly accepted the responsibility and opportunity to rebuild this nation. When pressed to break his army into guerrilla units and to continue the war indefinitely, Lee refused. He recognized that enough lives had been lost and that it was now time to end the Civil War and begin rebuilding the United States.

Lee took over the presidency of a near-bankrupt college in a backwater Virginia town and there became one of the leading educational pioneers in the history of this country. He revamped the curriculum in ways that were unheard of in this country, and emphasized practical curricula in the areas of business and engineering. Further, he was among the first in this country to recognize and emphasize the importance of teaching Spanish to the future leaders of this country.

While Lee concentrated his time in his later years on developing and rehabilitating the youth of the South, he continued to counsel his former comrades and friends to avoid bitterness and to get on with the remainder of their lives. At the earliest opportunity, he sought to be reinstated as a voting citizen of the United States and encouraged his friends to do likewise. More than any other single man, Robert E. Lee was responsible for the relatively peaceful post-Civil War era. The quality of this man and his impact is seen, not in how he lived with success, but rather how he lived in defeat.

Noah Webster and Books

The long daylight hours were never long enough to get the work done. Even though there were two brothers besides himself to help their father, the farm took all their strength and energy.

This was a great pity, thought Noah, because there were so many other things in the world as important as farming. Books and reading, for example. Although he had probably never seen more than a dozen books in his life, Noah Webster liked reading. He could think for hours about words and their meaning. A printed page was to him exciting new country. But how could he explore this new country when there were always animals to feed, corn to hoe, tools to mend or sharpen every waking moment? Only when darkness shut down at last could he hope to spend a few moments by the candle in the kitchen, or in his bedroom, reading whatever he could lay his hands on.

His brothers, Abram and Charles, did not agree with him about this. When he read in the bedroom at night, they only grunted and asked him to blow out the candle. But their small, wiry middle brother was not easily diverted. Shading the light with his hand, he plowed earnestly down whatever page he happened to be reading.

Life Is Tremendous

by Charles T. Jones
Recommended by: John M. Wells, Jr.

This is truly the most inspirational book I have ever read (after the Bible). The author describes the seven laws of leadership which, if followed, will surely lead to greater happiness and a more productive life.

By focusing on positive and pleasant thoughts, we gradually change our attitude to the point that life gets better and better, because we cause it to happen. Our own perception of life makes the difference.

God blesses us with struggle, because, when we struggle, we stretch ourselves a little further and thereby gain strength. Without problems and difficulties, our lives are meaningless.

My favorite law is the FOURTH LAW OF LEADERSHIP which tells us that we must "give to get". . . . We must learn that when we give of ourselves without waiting for something in return, we are actually overflowing our lives with good and wholesome thinking. Because of the power of (self) love, we gradually begin to gather good things in return. . . .

Then there is the SIXTH LAW OF LEADERSHIP: FLEXIBLE PLANNING. It means: "whatever can go wrong . . . will go wrong! Plan on your plan going wrong so that you are ready with an alternate plan. Do you know that a lot of people are miserable because they expect everything to go right, and so I'm jubilant all the time!" he writes. "The mark of a man who is growing in his understanding that things go wrong to make us more right. God never breaks a man down with problems except to build him up."

Life Is Tremendous will give you a warm glow because of the love and happiness that flows from chapter to chapter.

The Note Book of Elbert Hubbard

by Elbert Hubbard
Recommended by: Dail West, President, Westco, Inc.,

Montaigne said, "I quote others only the better to express myself." Elbert Hubbard's notebook is enriched with hundreds of choice quotations – for example: "The vintage of wisdom is to know that rest is rust and that real life is love, laughter, and work." "Do unto others as though you were the others," and, "Initiative is doing the right thing without being told."

Elbert Hubbard coined a Life of Love, Laughter and Work, achieving much in literature, art, philosophy and business. His *Note Book* is a collection of epigrams, short essays and preachments. They are as pertinent today as they were when written or collected some sixty years ago.

His "Message to Garcia" is a classic one that makes Hubbard remembered by so many. Here is an excerpt from the closing paragraph:

"My heart goes out to the man who does his work when the 'boss' is away, as well as when he is at home. And the man who, when given a letter for Garcia, quietly takes the message, without asking any idiotic questions, and with no lurking intention of chucking it into the nearest sewer, or of doing aught else but deliver it, never gets 'laid off,' nor has to go on a strike for higher wages. Civilization is one long, anxious search for just such individuals. Anything such a man asks shall be granted. He is wanted in every city, town and village – in every office, shop, store and factory. The world cries out for such: he is needed and needed badly – the man who can 'Carry a Message to Garcia.'"

The Truth about You

by Arthur F. Miller and Ralph T. Mattson
Recommended by: John L. West, President, National Equipment & Mold Corporation

The Truth about You is required reading for all those who have a desire to fulfill any part of their destiny—for which they were specifically created.

Arthur Miller and Ralph Mattson do not propose a new behavioral theory. They describe a phenomenon that is clearly and consistently demonstrable—and immediately applicable to your specific situation and needs, and mine.

The reason for my enthusiasm and excitement over *The Truth about You* is that it presents the solution to the problems represented by all of the below. It is not only evident that each of us possesses a unique and meaningful design of our own, but that it can be identified! It is true that:

"A surprising number of people are in situations that can be described as unfulfilling or joyless."

"Many people feel they are nobodies and almost desperately want to be somebodies."

"Thousands of young people are accused of not having direction in their lives . . . but do not know how to find it."

"YOU DO NOT HAVE TO TRY AND THEN FAIL IN ORDER TO REALIZE THAT YOU HAVE BEEN CLIMBING THE WRONG LADDER."

Confessions of an Advertising Man

by David Ogilvy
Recommended by: Somers H. White, CPAE
Professional Speaker

David Ogilvy was probably the first man ever to graduate from Oxford who became a chef. Later he became head of Ogilvy Mather, one of the five largest advertising agencies in the world. He was exalted as a writer of quality copy.

In his book, *Confessions of an Advertising Man*, he told how after graduating from Oxford he went to work as a chef at the Hotel Majestic in Paris under Monsieur Pitard, the head chef.

He wrote, "I saw him fire three pastry chefs in a month for the same crime: they can't make the caps on their brioches rise evenly." Mr. Gladstone would have applauded such ruthlessness: he said the first essential of a Prime Minister was to be a good butcher.

I find that most people, including me, wait too long to make the decisions they know should be made. In my opinion, the hardest thing in management is firing somebody. You have to learn how to be a good butcher in management and in your own personal life if you are going to be effective. You have to get rid of deadwood and change bad habits.

A Time for Action

by William E. Simon
Recommended by: Allan Willey

I don't have to remind you that this is a fast paced world we live in. Instant coffee, up-to-the-minute news coverage, and motivational fixes are part of everyday life.

It is refreshing and thought-provoking to take a step aside and consider where this fast pace is taking us. William E. Simon is a very successful businessman who also served in Washington as U.S. Secretary of the Treasury. He is one of the few men to enter politics and still retain a clear perspective on the workings of the Government and how it affects every American. That does not mean to say *A Time for Action* is a "heavy" book, as Mr. Simon writes clearly and concisely.

The message comes through loud and clear that the success of this country was based on freedom, initiative, capitalism and free enterprise. These features are being thwarted by a Government which has become all too pervasive, plus a tendency among the citizens to demand protection and handouts. A country as diversified as the U.S. will never run perfectly. However, the pendulum has swung from hard work, thrift and respect for fellow citizens to being treated as helpless, self-indulgent infants who need a federal nanny to look after us at every waking moment.

The book stirs patriotism and the need for all to get involved. The catchy cover comment gets right to the heart of it:

"If not us–who?"
"If not now–when?"

The Way of the Bull

by Leo Buscaglia
Recommended by: Charley Willey, CPAE
Professional Speaker, Humorist

The book, *The Way of the Bull*, by Leo Buscaglia has been one of the most moving books of my reading experience. It is a book that deals with his travels throughout the uttermost parts of the world and his involvement in the lives of the people he met while on this trip. The underlying thought in the entire writing is that LOVE is a universal process–that it knows no ethnic or racial barriers–that it is a universal quality of life and a universal need in life. By the mystical processes of human love, artificial barriers dissolve and people are one and the same as a part of the grandiose creation of Almighty God. As I read the book, it occurred to me that every major religion in the world has tried to convey this philosophy–that such qualities as empathy, forbearance, compassion, and warmth are not only essential to human happiness, but essential to human survival. We have made love such a complex experience that it is often robbed of its beauty. That simplicity is of the essence as our lives touch other lives and are strengthened by both giving and receiving.

Try Giving Yourself Away

by David Dunn
Recommended by: Dan Williams,
President, Williams Enterprises

One of my favorite books is *Try Giving Yourself Away*. It has been a pleasure to share this book with our children as well as with close friends.

This little book is a great "how-to" and "what-to-do" for people with a giving nature who want to put their Christian principles to work in a very practical way. Pray for the hungry family, but do bring them a bag of groceries as well!

"It is so easy to confuse our daily busyness with our daily business. Many of us earn our living in business, but waste much of the rest of our time on busyness that profits us little.

"Time was not created merely to be consumed in working and worrying, rushing for trains, and dashing to appointments. It was intended to be used in 'the pursuit of happiness,' as our discerning forefathers phrased it in the Declaration of Independence. True, we would find it hard to be happy if we did not work, and earn enough to live on, but beyond that, the aim of all of us should be to both *give* and *get* the greatest possible enjoyment from every sixty seconds of our lives.

"In terms of downright happiness, it is my experience that the returns-per-minute from *giving* are far greater than the returns from *getting*."

Inspirational Thoughts for Every Day

by Harold Blake Walker

Recommended by: Dr. Carl S. Winters, CPAE, Lecture Staff, General Motors Corporation

To me, the poet was right who said, "books are ladders up which climb human hearts to heights sublime."

When I moved to Chicago forty years ago, I discovered the beautiful item that Dr. Walker wrote for each issue of the *Chicago Tribune*. I bought the *Tribune* because of that item. Some ten years ago, with the help of his marvelous wife, he took the choicest of these daily thoughts and put them together in this beautiful book. Dr. Walker knows the poets "who pack truth close and make it portable." Dr. Walker knows the novelist who is the competent diagnostician to anyone who would help to heal the hurt of the world. He also knows the biographer who lets us see how high men may rise or how low they may fall. With incredible insight and will, he has chosen material from each of them to develop his biblical text of the day, concluding with a brief prayer at the end of each item.

Struggling with ill health and constantly in pain, Robert Louis Stevenson once said, "I must get out my wings." To him, a part of his wings was the books he read and the books he wrote. Some verse writer said, "He danced along the dingy days and this bequest of wings, was but a book, what liberty a loosen spirit brings." For one of my daily attachment of wings, I use Dr. Harold Blake Walker's marvelous book. He has chosen a beautiful editorial in it for every day in the entire year. It helps me to remove the world's slow stain from my mind and set my feet again upon the track to truth and joy.

Love, Acceptance and Forgiveness

by Jerry Cook and Stanley Baldwin
Recommended by: Leo Wisniewski, Football Player, Indianapolis Colts

This book centers on how God's principles of love, acceptance and forgiveness can revolutionize our marriages, our personal relationships and our relationship with God.

"Truth must be communicated to people, and that is accomplished primarily through simple, direct teaching of God's Word. The place to begin is to teach people who they are in Jesus–positional truth. Who am I? I'm more than simply a sinner saved. What does saved mean? What are the implications of that? Ephesians is great on this.

"Once a person begins to understand who he is and what he has, he will try the concepts out. When this process gets under way, the pastor will have to run to keep up with people instead of always trying to cook up some way to get them moving.

"I am convinced that pure, raw, direct exposure to the Word of God will absolutely change people's lives. In fact, many pastors would do their congregations a favor if they would stop trying to preach, sit down, open the Bible, and read it aloud. You can bet that 90 percent of the people aren't reading it for themselves."

Showmanship for Magicians

by Dariel Fitzkee
Recommended by: John Wolfe, CPAE
Author, Professional Speaker

It happened exactly 40 years ago. I was attending Dartmouth at the time, and also doing a magic act at various resort hotels throughout New England.

Like most magicians, I'd always concentrated on the tricks rather than the audience. The object, I'd been taught, was to "fool" the spectators. If they didn't catch on the secret, you were a hit. That was the conventional wisdom among tricksters generally.

But *Showmanship for Magicians* totally destroyed that myth. A magician is an entertainer, Dariel Fitzkee insisted. The "puzzles" aren't that important, he said – nor, in fact, are magic tricks all that amazing, anyway. In an age of color TV, space travel and micro-computer chips (putting it in today's terms), what's so remarkable about finding a rabbit in a hat? Nothing! But if people derive pleasure and benefit from a performance, then the entertainment has succeeded. The crucial point is how you "tune in" to the audience. And the book went on to describe how to bring this about.

Thinking back now, I realize that this approach to magic – and to speaking and to selling and to daily living – has affected my entire life. In fact, it's influenced my own writings as well. In the Introduction to my book, *Miracle Platform Power*, I say in part: "What you say and how you say it are totally unimportant – except in terms of how your message is received by the audience."

Love or Perish

by Dr. Smiley Blanton
Recommended by: Bill Woodruff,
Certified Speaking Professional

Love or Perish, written by Dr. Blanton, the psychiatrist who was born in 1881, preceded so many recent books that deal with solving the problems of human beings, that it can be considered a "source" book.

With my own scientific training as a Chemical Engineer, I was deeply impressed by Dr. Blanton's logical approach to that which "heals, cultivates, protects and inspires." The book contains little in the way of empty phrases, but rather concerns itself with concepts, ideas and conclusions drawn from forty years of listening, "while people of all ages and classes told me of their hopes and fears, their likes and dislikes, and of what they considered good or bad about themselves and the world around them."

I was first drawn into the book by a brief summary of the work of my namesake Lorande Woodruff, the Yale University biologist showing how one cell has a rejuvenating influence upon another without an actual union of the two.

Then I was impressed by how Major-General S. S. P. Thorat used love to overcome hate with 22,000 enraged and hysterical prisoners of war at Panmunjom.

Only as I first read this book twenty-five years ago did it dawn on me the tremendous impact that LOVE has in human relationships throughout life. It is many times more pervasive and influential than the popularized man/woman sexual love.

The Americanization of Edward Bok

by Edward Bok

Recommended by: Benjamin N. Woodson, Insurance Exec., Recipient of National Assn. of Life Underwriters' John Newton Russell Award

So many books have influenced me that I really could not name any one which influenced me "more than any other." But if pressed, I think I would name *The Americanization of Edward Bok*." He was a gentleman of great distinction who was born in Holland, brought to this country at approximately age seven, had to adjust to a new country and a new world, a new language, and new culture and customs – and did so! He did it so very successfully that he became a personage of great distinction in America in the first and second decades of the twentieth century, particularly in the editorial and literary world. And his book above named was a non-fiction best seller for most of a decade, and was widely read and widely discussed.

I cannot give any quotation from the book, which I read with eagerness and excitement about 1927, '28 or '29. The latter year (1929) in which my own twenty-first birthday occured, and in that era, and at that time of my life, Mr. Bok's philosophy did indeed influence my life greatly; and from that year on, and profoundly so.

Dr. Derek Bok, who serves today as the president of Harvard University, is the grandson of Edward Bok.

Dexter Yager and Books

Some books that helped me are:

1. *Acres of Diamonds*
2. *The Magic of Believing*
3. *The Magic of Thinking Big*
4. *The Holy Bible*
5. *How to be Rich* by J. Paul Getty was a book that helped change my life. First it taught, and more important backed up thoughts, I believed but couldn't put my finger on until I saw it in print.
6. *Life Is Tremendous*
7. *The Success System that Never Fails*
8. *As I See It* by J. Paul Getty is a book that helped me realize men who succeed are basically hard working, honest men of principals. In this book J. Paul Getty is transparent as to honestly evaluating his life, his marriages, his success and failures, his good points and bad points. He speaks honestly of his hurts and makes a person realize he was only human, but he followed his beliefs and chased his dreams.
9. *See You at the Top* by Zig Ziglar teaches basics of sales that I had never been taught, but needed to know to reach the success I've achieved.

Between Parent and Child

by Haim Ginott
Recommended by: Dave Yoho,
CPAE, Certified Speaking Professional

Dr. Ginott's beautiful and unabashed approach to "inter-personal" language as used between parent and child is a treatise on where the management style and language of most adults probably originates.

If it comes as no surprise that our grammar and much of our base language is established prior to age five and reinforced by age eleven, then Dr. Ginott's book establishes what's wrong with what we have learned.

Ginott's examples of parent-child language introduce burning examples of how we as managers tend to use reaction language.

He also examines the concept of permitting others the right to their feelings and, while he is dealing with the parent-child relationship, it is obvious that this helps you understand management development and tolerate the behavior of others.

In the aftermath of reading this book, I chose it as my number three recommendation for clients and those attending my management seminars.

It is almost undeniable that whatever you were then, coupled with whatever you have been exposed to, strongly influences what you are now.

Thank you Haim Ginott!

Great Thoughts On Reading

John Henry Newman on What to Read

Some one will say to me, perhaps our youth shall not be corrupted. We will dispense with all general or national literature whatever, if it be so exceptional; we will have a Christian literature of our own, as pure, as true as the Jewish. You cannot have it. . . . From the nature of the case, if literature is to be made a study of human nature, you cannot have a Christian literature. It is a contradiction in terms to attempt a sinless literature of sinful men. You may gather together something very great and high, something higher than any literature ever was; and when you have done so, you will find that it is not literature at all. You will simply have left the delineation of man, as such, and have substituted for it, as far as you have had anything to substitute that of man, as he is or might be, under special advantages. Give up the study of man, as such, if so it must be; but say you do so. Do not say you are studying him, his history, his mind, and his heart, when you are studying something else. Man is a being of genius, passion, intellect, conscience, power. He exercises his great gifts in various ways – in great deeds, in great thoughts, in heroic acts, in hateful crimes. . . . Literature records them all to the life.

Read and Re-Read

Charles Haddon Spurgeon

Master those books you have. Read them thoroughly. Bathe in them until they saturate you. READ AND RE-READ them, masticate them, and digest them. Let them go into your very self. Peruse a good book several times, and make notes and analyses of it. A student will find that his mental constitution is more affected by one book thoroughly mastered than by twenty books which he has merely skimmed, lapping at them, as the classic proverb puts it, "As the dogs drink of Nilus." Little learning and much pride come of hasty reading. Books may be piled on the brain till it cannot work. Some men are disabled from thinking by their putting meditation away for the sake of much reading. They gorge themselves with book-matter, and become mentally dyspeptic.

The foundation of knowledge must be laid by reading. General principles must be had from books; which, however, must be brought to the test of real life. In conversation you never get a system. What is said upon a subject is to be gathered from a hundred people. The parts which a man gets thus are at such a distance from each other that he never attains to a full view.

–Dr. S. Johnson

Thoughts about Reading

Always have a book at hand, in the parlor, on the table, for the family; a book of condensed thoughts and striking anecdotes, of sound maxims and truthful apothegms. It will impress on your mind a thousand valuable suggestions, and teach our children a thousand lessons of truth and duty. Such a book is a casket of jewels for your household.

–Tryon Edwards

When you read the best books, you will have as the guests of your mind the best thoughts of the best men.

–Grenville Kleiser

Every man who knows how to read has it in his power to magnify himself, to multiply the ways in which he exists, to make his life full, significant and interesting.

–Aldous Huxley

A man ought to read just as inclination leads him; for what he reads as a task will do him little good. A young man should read five hours in a day, and so may acquire a great deal of knowledge.

–Samuel Johnson

If thou wouldst profit by thy reading, read humbly, simply, honestly, and not desiring to win a reputation for learning.

–Thomas à Kempis

Be Constantly on Guard
Thomas Jefferson

"Three great and influential books of the Eighteenth Century interested Jefferson and yet disturbed him. One was Montesquieu's *Spirit of Laws*, another was David Hume's *History of England*, the third was Blackstone's *Commentaries on the Laws of England*. Each was a masterpiece of its kind. Each conveyed ideas of the greatest importance and value. Each was in Jefferson's library and each was carefully studied by him. There could be no question of denying these books their rightful place in the making of American opinion. On the other hand, each work incorporated doctrines which Jefferson felt to be inimical to the ideals in which he believed and on which he felt the republic to be founded. The fact that he respected these books was no reason for allowing their influence to go unchallenged. How Jefferson dealt with each of the three books illustrates his conception of the positive obligation of a believer in liberty.

"Jefferson's opinion of Montesquieu was decidedly mixed. The *Spirit of Laws*, he wrote in 1790, 'contains indeed a great number of political truths; but almost an equal number of political heresies: so that the reader must be constantly on his guard.'"

–Arthur Beaston
Windsor Lectures, 1955

Greats on Reading

A proper and judicious system of reading is of the highest importance. Two things are necessary in perusing the mental labours of others; namely, not to read too much, and to pay great attention to the nature of what you do read. Many persons peruse books for the express and avowed purpose of consuming time; and this class of readers forms by far the majority of what are termed the reading public; others, again, read with the laudable anxiety of being made wiser; and when this object is not attained, the disappointment may generally be attributed either to the habit of reading too much, or of paying insufficient attention to what falls under their notice.

–Blakey

Who is he that is now wholly overcome with idleness, or otherwise involved in a labyrinth of worldly care, troubles, and discontents, that will not be much lightened in his mind by reading of some enticing story, true or feigned, where, as in a glass, he shall observe what our forefathers have done; the beginnings, ruins, falls, periods of commonwealths, private men's actions, displayed to the life, &c. Plutarch therefore calls them, secundas mensas et bellaria, the second course and junkets, because they were usually read at noblemen's feasts.

–Robert Burton

Ashley Montagu on Reading

Author, Educator

The initiation of the habit of reading early in the life of the child can be made an exciting experience, which should, of course, be a pleasurable one for the parents as well as for the child. It can be among the most delightful, sharing, and enhancing of encounters. It should, therefore, never be approached as a chore or a duty, for perfunctoriness does not greatly recommend itself to the child. Children who are read to as a duty will receive an uninviting impression of the purpose of reading. Children enjoy nothing more than being read to, when the reader enjoys the reading and communicates his enthusiasm to the child. "Tell me a story" is the universal appeal of the child, and is, of course, the principal reason for the enduring popularity of children's books. Such books as Lewis Carroll's *Alice in Wonderland*, Kenneth Graham's *The Wind in the Willows*, Antoine Saint-Exupéry's *The Little Prince*, E. B. White's *Charlotte's Web*, Munro Leaf's *Ferdinand the Bull*, though written for children, enjoy their greatest readership among adults. And the reason for this is not far to seek: it is the nostalgic delight that we take in the recovery of the world of childhood, the wonderland, the land of dreams, the recreation of myth.

The reading of stories to children is not only an important educational experience for the child, but also an opportunity for firmer bonding between parent and child: an opportunity to answer all sorts of questions that come to the child's mind, and to raise new ones. The shared experience in storytelling, of reading as it were together, constitutes the best introduction to reading even before the child can spell.

Francis Bacon on Reading

In the essay "Of Truth" he writes: "The inquiry of truth, which is the love-making or wooing of it; the knowledge of truth, which is the praise of it; and the belief of truth, which is the enjoying of it, is the sovereign good of human natures." In books "we converse with the wise, as in action with fools." That is, if we know how to select our books. "Some books are to be tasted," reads a famous passage, "others to be swallowed, and some few to be chewed and digested"; all these groups forming, no doubt, an infinitesimal portion of the oceans and cataracts of ink in which the world is daily bathed and poisoned and drowned.

Sir John Hershel on Reading

If I were to pray for a taste which should stand me instead under every variety of circumstances, and be a source of happiness and cheerfulness to me through life, and a shield against its ills, however things might go amiss and the world frown upon me, it would be a taste for reading. I speak of it of course only as a worldly advantage, and not in the slightest degree as superseding or derogating from the highest office and surer and stronger panoply of religious principles, but as a taste, an instrument, and a mode of pleasurable gratification. Give a man this taste and the means of gratifying it, and you can hardly fail of making a happy man, unless, indeed, you put into his hands a most perverse selection of books.

Thoughts about Reading

Every man who knows how to read has it in his power to magnify himself, to multiply the ways in which he exists, to make his life full, significant and interesting.

–Aldous Huxley

Three days' neglect of study leaves one's conversation flavorless.

–Chinese proverb

The first time I read an interesting book, it is to me just as if I had gained a new friend; when I read over a book I have perused before, it resembles the meeting with an old one.

–Oliver Goldsmith

If the crowns of the world were laid at my feet in exchange for my love of reading, I would spurn them all.

–Fenelon

In science, read by preference the newest works; in literature, the oldest. The classic literature is always modern.

–Edward Bulwer-Lytton

The Personal Library

by Dr. Orison S. Marden

A great help in obtaining the knowledge which sinks in, springs up, and bears efficient fruit, comes from owning good books. Much of the wisdom which people possess probably comes from things which they read and re-read many times in their schoolbooks. The sense of hurry engendered by the knowledge that a book must be returned to the public library at a certain time is extremely detrimental, if not fatal, to that absorption of its meaning from which alone can come power or restful pleasure. Therefore, have a library of your own. It does not need to be a large library. Nearly all America's greatest men and women read but few books when young, but these few they read so exhaustively, and digested so thoroughly, that their spirit, purpose, and principles become a part of the readers' very souls, the dynamos which moved their lives to great ends.

What luxury, never enjoyed by former monarchs of the earth, does a thinker now find in books! There is no spot on earth so dejecting, poverty-stricken, or distressing that a trained mind cannot only summon the grandest characters that live in history, but he can also find them at their best; they will give him their best thoughts, their best moods, and finest philosophy.

How to Read

Frederick Harrison
1913

When will men understand that the reading of great books is a faculty to be acquired, not a natural gift, as least not to those who are spoiled by our current education and habits of life? "This will kill that," the last great poet might have said of the first circulating library. An insatiable appetite for new novels makes it as hard to read a masterpiece as it seems to a Parisian boulevardier to live in a quiet country. Until a man can truly enjoy a draft of clear water bubbling from a mountain side, his taste is in an unwholesome state. And so he who finds the Heliconian spring insipid should look to the state of his nerves. Putting aside the iced air of the difficult mountain top of epic, tragedy, or psalm, there are some simple pieces which may serve as an unerring test of a healthy or a vicious taste for imaginative work. If the *Cid*, the *Vita Nuova*, the *Canterbury Tales*, Shakespear's *Sonnets*, and *Lycidas* pall on a man; if he can not for Malory's *Morte d'Arthur* and the *Red Cross Knight*; if he thinks *Crusoe* and the *Vicar* books for the young; if he thrill not with *The Ode to the West Wind*, and *The Ode to a Grecian Urn*; if he have no stomach for *Christabel* or the lines written on *The Wye above Tintern Abbey*, he should fall on his knees and pray for a cleanlier and quieter spirit.

How Shall We Read?

by George C. Lorimer, 1896

What method is best? What rules are most entitled to our confidence? Goethe says that for eighteen years he had tried to define and acquire this art and had not been remarkably successful. And Richter, in similar perplexity, inquires, "Does more depend on the order in which the meats follow each other or on the digestion of them?" Who can tell? Even in the assimilation of food, ice-cream logically seems to follow soup and meats, and, if taken at too early a stage in the proceedings, might interfere with the enjoyment of the repast as well as seriously disturb the functions of nature.

Every one must carefully feel his way to his own method, and if he is in earnest, he will ultimately evolve one that will at least serve him as a pair of crutches, even if it cannot do duty as wings.

But though I am different as to the formulating of specific rules, there are several precautions I venture to make, and the first is, Avoid aimlessness and irreverence in reading. Be sure to have a purpose, and let it be approached with becoming gravity.

What Is a Book?

Earl Prevette

It is what someone has seen, felt, imagined, experienced, or discovered, expressed in words to convey to you this knowledge and information. Therefore, by reading you come in contact with the great minds of the past and of the present. You learn to comprehend with Shakespeare, to reason with Plato to meditate with Emerson, to observe with Burroughs, to weigh and to concentrate with Bacon, to think with Socrates, to share Lincoln's compassion, to feel the stir and the drama of Churchill, and generally to profit spiritually from the minds deeper and broader than your own.

What to Read?

Earl Prevette

I do not tell you what books to read specifically. That is something that your own taste must determine. In your diet, you eat what you like and abstain from what you don't like. The same is true of books. One type of book will appeal to you and another will not. The all-important thing is to be interested in books. Books themselves will form your taste if you form the habit of reading them. But I want to make one suggestion with which I am sure you will agree. Read books that interest you and not because it is considered correct to read them. If the classics are too heavy for you, forget them. If the philosophers bore you, dismiss them. If great poetry leaves you cold, leave it alone. If great novels fall short of your expectations, there are ten thousand others at your beck and call. Read for joy of reading and not to conform to vicarious acclaim. Meanwhile, remember that good reading broadens the appreciation of all literature and almost surely you will turn later to authors who seem a little remote to you now.

Bibliography

Alcoholics Anonymous. Alcoholics Anonymous World Services.

Allen, James. *As a Man Thinketh*. Executive Books, 1984.

Andelin, Aubrey. *Man of Steel & Velvet*. Bantam.

Apenszlak, Jacob, ed. *Black Book of Polish Jewry*. Fertig, 1982.

Armbruster, Wally. *Noodles Du Jour*. Concordia, 1976.

Assagioli, Roberto. *The Act of Will*. Penguin, 1974.

Aurelius, Marcus. *Meditations*. Penguin, 1964.

Baker, Russell. *Growing Up*. Corqdon and Weed, 1982.

Bettger, Frank. *How I Raised Myself from Failure to Success in Selling*. Cornerstone, 1975.

Black, Joe. *Ain't Nobody Better Than You*. 1983.

Blanchard, Kenneth, and Johnson, Spencer, *One Minute Manager*. Berkley, 1983.

Bolt, Robert. *A Man for All Seasons*. Random House.

Bok, Edward. *Americanization of Edward Bok*. Greenwood, 1972.

Brande, Dorothy. *Wake Up and Live*. Cornerstone, 1980.

Bristol, Claude. *The Magic of Believing*. Pocket Books.

Burden, Billy. *When the Going Gets Tough*. Revell.

Buscaglia, Leo. *Love*. Fawcett, 1982.

Buscaglia, Leo. *The Way of the Bull*. Slack, Inc., 1974.

Capote, Truman. *Other Voices, Other Rooms*. Random House.

Carnegie, Dale. *How to Develop Self Confidence and Influence People by Public Speaking*. Pocket Books, 1977.

Carnegie, Dale. *How to Stop Worrying and Start Living*. Pocket Books, 1981.

Carnegie, Dale. *How to Win Friends and Influence People*. Pocket Books, 1982.

Caro, Robert. *Power Broker: Robert Moses & the Fall of New York*. Random House, 1975.

Clason, George. *The Richest Man in Babylon*. Hawthorn Books, 1955.

Colson, Charles. *Born Again*. Bantam, 1976.
Colson, Charles. *Loving God*. Zondervan, 1983.
Conklin, Robert. *How to Get People to Do Things*. Ballantine, 1982.
Connor, Ralph. *The Sky Pilot*. Lightyear, 1976.
Cook, Jerry, and Baldwin, Stanley. *Love, Acceptance and Forgiveness*. Regal Books, 1979.
Cooper, Kenneth. *The Aerobics Program for Total Well-Being*. M. Evans & Co., 1982.
Cousins, Norman. *The Healing Heart*. Norton, 1983.
Cummings, Harold. *Prescription for Tomorrow.* Farnsworth, 1980.
Danforth, William. *I Dare You*. American Youth Foundation, 1980.
de Bono, Edward. *New Think*. Basic Books, 1968.
DeGreen, Keith. *Creating a Success Environment*. Summit Enterprises, 1979.
DeRopp, Robert. *The Master Game*. Dell, 1969.
DeSaint-Exupery, Antoine. *The Little Prince*.
Dobson, James. *Straight Talk to Men and Their Wives*. Word Books, 1980.
Douglas, Lloyd. *Magnificent Obsession*. Houghton Mifflin, 1938.
Drucker, Peter. *The Practice of Management*. Harper & Row, 1954.
Dumas, Alexandre. *The Three Musketeers*. Penguin, 1982.
Dunn, David. *Try Giving Yourself Away*. Prentice-Hall.
Durant, Will and Ariel. *The Lessons of History*. Simon & Schuster, 1968.
Edwards, William. *Ten Days to a Great New Life*. Wilshire.
Emery, Stewart. *Actualizations: You Don't Have to Rehearse to be Yourself*. Doubleday-Dolphin, 1978.
Fast, Howard. *Freedom Road*. Bantam, 1969.
Fineman, Irving. *Woman of Valor*, Simon & Schuster, 1961.
Fitzgerald, Edward. *Rubaijat of Omar Khayyan*.

Fitzgerald, Robert. *Ulysses.*
Fitzkee, Dariel. *Showmanship for Magicians.* Borden.
Flood, Charles. *Lee, The Last Years.* Houghton Mifflin, 1981.
Follett, Ken. *On Wings of Eagles.* Signet, 1984.
Foster, Richard. *Freedom of Simplicity.* Harper & Row, 1981.
Frankl, Victor, *Man's Search for Meaning.* Pocket Books, 1980.
Franklin, Benjamin. *Autobiography.* Random House, 1981.
Gallway, Timothy. *The Inner Game of Tennis.* Bantam, 1979.
Gardner, John. *Self-Renewal: The Individual and the Innovative Society.* Norton, 1983.
Getty, J. Paul. *How to Be Rich.* Jove, 1973.
Gibran, Kahlil. *The Prophet.* Knopf.
Gifford, Frank. *Gifford on Courage.* M. Evans & Co., 1976.
Gilson, Etienne. *Spirit of Medieval Philosophy.* Scribners
Gingrich, Newt. *Window of Opportunity.* St. Martins Press, 1984.
Ginott, Haim. *Between Parent and Child.* Avon, 1969.
Glosser, William. *Reality Theory.* Harper & Row, 1965.
Greenburg, Dan. *How to Make Yourself Miserable.* Institute for Rational-Emotive Therapy.
Greenleaf, Robert. *Servant Leadership.* Paulist, 1977.
Hill, Napoleon. *Grow Rich with Peace of Mind.* Fawcett, 1978.
Hill, Napoleon. *Laws of Success.* Success Unlimited, 1969.
Hill, Napoleon. *Think and Grow Rich.* Fawcett, 1979.
Hill, Napoleon, and Stone, W. Clement. *Success Through a Positive Mental Attitude.* Pocket Books, 1977.
Hubbard, Elbert. *The Note Book of Elbert Hubbard.* Petrocelli, 1980.
Hummel, Charles E. *Tyranny of Urgent.*

Huss, John. *Robert E. Lee, The Authorized Biography*. Zondervan, 1967.

Iacocca, Lee, and Novak, William. *Iacocca, an Autobiography*. Bantam, 1984.

Jampolsky, Gerald. *Love is Letting Go of Fear*. Bantam, 1982.

Jensen, Jay. *The Best of Sterling Sill*. Bookcraft, Inc.

Johnson, Paul. *Modern Times*. Harper & Row, 1983.

Jones, Charles. *Life Is Tremendous*. Tyndale House.

Joyce, James. *Ulysses*.

Kanin, Garson. *It Takes a Long Time to Become Young*. G. K. Hall, 1978.

Keller, James. *You Can Change the World*. Harper & Row.

Kinder, Jack Jr., Kinder, Gary, and Staubach, Roger. *Winning Strategies in Selling*. Prentice-Hall, 1981

Koestler, Arthur. *Darkness at Noon*. Macmillan, 1941.

Korda, Michael. *Success!* Random House, 1977.

Krause, David. *Peak Performance*. Prentice-Hall, 1980.

Kroc, Ray. *Grinding It Out: The Making of McDonald's*. Berkley, 1982.

Kyne, Peter. *The Go-Getter*. Holt, Rinehart & Winston.

Laidlaw, Alexander, ed. *The Man from Margaree. Writings & Speeches of M. M. Coady*. McLelland & Stewart, 1971.

Lakein, Alan. *How to Get Control of Your Time and Your Life*. NAL, 1974.

Lewis, C. S. *Mere Christianity*. Macmillan, 1978.

Lewis, C. S. *Screwtape Letters*. Revell, 1978.

Lewis, C. S. *The Weight and the Glory*. Macmillan, 1980.

Lewis, Sinclair. *Arrowsmith*. NAL.

Lewis, Sinclair. *Babbitt*. NAL.

Lindbergh, Anne. *Gift from the Sea*. Random House.

Lubbock, John. *The Pleasures of Life*. Richard West, 1973.

Maltz, Maxwell. *Psycho-Cybernetics*. Pocket Books.

Manchester, William. *The Last Lion*. Little, Brown & Co., 1983.

Mandino, Og. *The Greatest Miracle in the World*. Bantam, 1977.

Mandino, Og. *The Greatest Salesman in the World*. Bantam, 1978.

Mandino, Og. *The Greatest Secret in the World*. Bantam, 1978.

Marshall, Catherine. *A Man Called Peter*. Avon 1971.

Maslow, Abraham. *Motivation and Personality*. Harper & Row, 1970.

Massie, Robert and Susie. *Journey*. Knopf, 1975.

McCullough, David. *Mornings on Horseback*. Simon & Schuster, 1982.

McDowell, Josh. *More Than a Carpenter*. Tyndale House, 1977.

Melville, Herman. *Moby Dick*. Biblio Distributors, 1977

Neville. *Resurrection*. De Vorss, 1966.

Nightingale, Earl. *This Is Earl Nightingale*. Nightingale-Conant, 1983.

Nirenberg, Jesse. *Getting Through to People*. Prentice-Hall, 1968.

Ogilvy, David. *Confessions of an Advertising Man*. Atheneum, 1980.

Osborne, Cecil. *Art of Understanding Yourself*. Word Books.

Ouchi, William. *Theory Z—How American Business Can Meet the Japanese Challenge*. Addison-Wesley, 1981.

Paulus, Trina. *Hope for the Flowers*. Paulist Press, 1972.

Peale, Norman Vincent. *Enthusiasm Makes the Difference*. Fawcett, 1978.

Peale, Norman Vincent. *Positive Imaging*. Revell, 1981.

Peale, Norman Vincent. *The Power of Positive Thinking*. Revell, 1966.

Peale, Norman Vincent. *Tough Minded Optimist*. Fawcett, 1979.

Peck, Richard. *Something for Joey*. Bantam, 1978.

Peck, Scott. *The Road Less Traveled*. Simon & Schuster, 1980.

Peters, Thomas, and Waterman, Robert Jr. *In Search of Excellence*. Warner, 1983.
Phillips, J. B. *Your God is Too Small*. Hazelden.
Piper, Watty. *The Little Engine That Could*. Scholastic, 1979.
Porter, Jane. *The Scottish Chiefs*. Scribner, 1982.
Powell, John. *Unconditional Love*. Argus, 1978.
Proctor, Bob. *Born Rich*. McCrary Pub.
Rand, Ayn. *Atlas Shrugged*. NAL.
Ries, Al, and Trout, Jack. *Positioning: The Battle for Your Mind.* Warner, 1982.
Roth, Charles. *The Secrets of Closing*. Prentice-Hall, 1982.
Schindler, John. *How To Live 365 Days a Year*. Fawcett, 1978.
Schuller, Robert. *Move Ahead with Possibility Thinking*. Jove, 1973.
Schuller, Robert. *Tough Times Never Last, But Tough People Do*. Thomas Nelson, 1983.
Schwartz, David. *The Magic of Self Direction*. Cornerstone, 1975.
Schwartz, David. *The Magic of Thinking Big.* Cornerstone, 1962.
Scott, Dru. *How to Put More Time in Your Life.* NAL, 1982.
Scott, M. and Pelliccioni, L. Jr. *Don't Choke: How Athletes Can Become Winners*. Prentice-Hall.
Shaklee, Forrest. *Reflections on a Philosophy*. Benjamin Co.
Sheehan, George. *Running & Being–The Total Experience.* Simon & Schuster.
Simon, William. *A Time for Action*. Berkley, 1982.
Smalley, Gary. *For Better or for Best*. Zondervan, 1982.
Stanford, Miles. *The Green Letters–Principles of Spiritual Growth*. Zondervan, 1975.
Stedman, Ray. *Authentic Christianity*. Word
Steil, Lyman. *Your Most Enchanted Listener*. Harper & Row, 1946.

Stein, Ben. *Bunkhouse Logic*. Avon, 1981.

Stigum, Marsha. *Money Market Book*. Dow Jones-Irwin, 1983.

Stone, Irving. *Love Is Eternal*. NAL, 1972.

Sullivan, Frank. *The Critical Path to Sales Success*. Research and Review Service of America, 1980.

Sweetland, Ben. *I Can*. Wilshire, 1976.

Swindoll, Charles. *Encourage Me*. Multnomah Press, 1982.

Swindoll, Charles. *Growing Strong in the Seasons of Life*. Multnomah Press, 1983.

Swindoll, Charles. *Improving Your Serve*. Word, 1981.

Swindoll, Charles. *Strengthening Your Grip*. Word, 1982.

Tolkien, J. R. *Lord of the Rings*. Fotonovel, 1979.

Tolstoy, Leo. *Anna Karenina*. Bantam.

Tournier, Paul. *The Healing of Persons*. Harper & Row, 1983.

Tozer, A. W. *The Knowledge of the Holy*. Harper & Row, 1978

Twain, Mark. *Adventures of Huckleberry Finn*. Penguin, 1983.

Tzu, Lao. *The Way of Life*. NAL, 1955.

Von Mises, Ludwig. *Human Action: A Treatise on Economics*. Contemporary Books, 1966.

Waitley, Denis. *Seeds of Greatness*, Revell, 1983.

Walford, Roy. *Maximum Life Span*. Norton, 1983.

Watt, Leilani. *Caught in the Conflict*. Harvest House, 1984.

Weinberg, George. *Self Creation*. Avon, 1978.

Williams, Marjorie. *The Velveteen Rabbit*. Avon, 1983.

Williams, William Carlos. *Paterson*. Harper & Row.

Williamson, Porter. *Patton's Principles*. Simon & Schuster, 1982.

Wolfe, Thomas. *Look Homeward, Angel*. Scribner, 1982.

Ziglar, Zig. *See You at the Top*. Pelican, 1982.

One cardinal rule to remember in reading. You only get to keep and enjoy what you share and give away. If you aren't going to read with the purpose of sharing and giving, I suggest you give the book to someone who will share with you and you'll discover the power of books as you watch your friends grow through sharing with you. Perhaps the best idea would be to use the brain trust idea of *Think and Grow Rich* and both of you begin reading and sharing with each other. (You'd be surprised what could happen in your home life if you tried it there, too.)

–Charles "T" Jones

For additional reading lists or childrens reading contracts send a self-addressed, stamped envelop to:

Life Management Services, Inc.
Box 1044
Harrisburg, PA 17108
717-763-1950

A blessed companion is a book, – a book that, fitly chosen, is a lifelong friend, . . . a book that, at a touch, pours its heart into our own.

– Douglas Jerrold

The best effect of any book is that it excites the reader activity.

–Thomas Carlyle

The peace of great books be for you,
Stains of pressed clover leaves on pages,
Bleach of the light of years held in leather.

– Carl Sandburg, *For You*

When you read a classic, you do not see more in the book than you did before; you see more in *you* than there was before.

– Clifton Fadiman

I am a part of all that I have read.

– John Kieran

Show me the books he loves and I shall know/The man far better than through mortal friends.

– S. Weir Mitchell

There is a great deal of difference between an eager man who wants to read a book and the tired man who wants a book to read.

– G. K. Chesterton